Conflict Management
for Libraries

STRATEGIES FOR A POSITIVE, PRODUCTIVE WORKPLACE

JACK G. MONTGOMERY
and
ELEANOR I. COOK

With Contributions by
Pat Wagner
and
Glenda Hubbard

AMERICAN LIBRARY ASSOCIATION
CHICAGO   2005

Printed on 50-pound white offset, a pH-neutral stock, and bound in 10-point cover stock by McNaughton & Gunn.

The paper used in this publication meets the minimum requirements of American National Standard for Information Sciences—Permanence of Paper for Printed Library Materials, ANSI Z39.48-1992. ⊚

Library of Congress Cataloging-in-Publication Data

Montgomery, Jack G.
    Conflict management for libraries : strategies for a positive, productive workplace / Jack G. Montgomery and Eleanor I. Cook ; with contributions from Patricia Wagner and Glenda Hubbard.
      p. cm.
    Includes bibliographical references and index.
    ISBN 0-8389-0890-X
    1. Library personnel management. 2. Conflict management. I. Cook, Eleanor I. II. Wagner, Patricia Jean. III. Hubbard, Glenda T. IV. Title.
    Z682.M655 2005
    023′.9—dc22   2004030722

Printed in the United States of America

09 08 07 06 05   5 4 3 2 1

CONTENTS

PREFACE
Why Write This Book?

WHEN WE WERE FIRST APPROACHED REGARDING THE POSSIBILITY OF WRITING a book about organizational conflict in libraries, we asked ourselves, *Why is this book necessary?* Multitudes of books on management practices and conflict resolution exist and are readily accessible. So why should yet another title be added to the pile?

Many of the theories and ideas expressed in this book actually came from a series of presentations and articles we created over the past six years. Time and again we would find ourselves at conferences and meetings listening to various discussions on all the hot library topics of the day. When those presentations were over, the conversation invariably would turn to dilemmas related to the staff we supervise, the colleagues we work with, and the administrators we aim to please on a daily basis. It became apparent that there was a professional need that was not being met. Like curious children behind the barn trying to learn the facts of life from equally uninformed playmates, we were struggling to understand managerial and interpersonal elements in the same haphazard fashion—in other words, not very effectively.

Because the majority of management tomes published today are written from a corporate point of view (that is, they assume the reader works in a commercial environment), librarians, most of whom work in the public sector, have to "translate" the advice and wisdom shared within those pages. We have used many of these sources as background information for this book and have performed that translation for our audience.

Our audience, specifically, is managers in libraries. We acknowledge that many of the personnel problems encountered in our little part of the world are not so different from any other business setting, but we also strive to address particular issues that are unique to libraries. Libraries have a culture that is based on long traditions that are distinct from corporate systems. Librarians have evolved from stern gatekeepers (imagine the large volumes of the past, chained to the reading stalls) to modern, accessible public servants. We keep our eye on the changing nature of our patrons' information needs far better than we do on the financial bottom line. Although we are still custodians of the intellectual and creative output of civilization, we now focus more on meeting the immediate needs of our users in a fast-changing environment. We believe our mission is a lofty, inspired public good, but our strategic plans are not based on stockholders' needs and profit margins.

We also recognize that this book is developed from an American viewpoint; ours is not an attempt to address libraries in an international sense, though we acknowledge and in fact address the challenges faced by globalization.

At a social gathering some years ago, Jack was engaged in a conversation with a fellow librarian and another colleague from the commercial sector. At one point, the business colleague remarked, "It must be great to work in a library; everything is so quiet and relaxed, and people don't raise their voices or get upset!" Jack and his librarian friend looked at each other incredulously and burst out laughing at the absurdity of this impression. Although not, on the surface, as volatile as some work environments, libraries are not immune to stress and conflict. In fact, that stereotype of the quiet, orderly place intensifies the troubles that simmer below the surface. It has been observed that libraries in several ways resemble the post office environment. The following are some similarities:

> The work often involves highly repetitive, detail-oriented tasks requiring long-term concentration. Additional pressures include production quotas; physically close, not always comfortable working conditions; and computer fatigue.

> There is often a top-heavy bureaucracy, which might foster feelings of alienation and psychological distance from the decision-making process, leading in turn to feelings of helplessness and lack of control over factors that affect one's life. Supervisors often feel isolated from administration and are indirectly encouraged to ignore all but the most heinous transgressions. Management training seminars usually address employee discipline. A typical statement workshop leaders might share with an assembled group of managers goes something like this: "All

I can say is, don't do anything that will get us [the university, the city, etc.] sued; we just might not be able to stand behind you. You could lose your job!" The effect of such a remark can be chilling. Sadly, administrators and human resource personnel may not be any more adept at handling conflict than inexperienced line or middle managers. This lack of support from above can be very frustrating.

Librarians and library staff work at tasks and develop job skills that have no direct correlation or application to other markets outside of libraries. The basic library science master's degree, like other professional degrees, is focused to serve a special constituency. Despite the fact that many librarians now work in the commercial sector, many library staff are connected to a certain geographic area because of family or personal obligations and are reluctant or unable to move on to other types of employment. In rural or remote regions, employment choices may be slim. Hence, not unlike what we hear about the postal system, staff can be left feeling trapped in a line of work they do not necessarily enjoy but have little in the way of options for transferring out.

In many library environments, although progressive management policies are emerging, the institutional culture has deeply ingrained civil service characteristics. Many librarians and their staffs are municipal, state, or federal employees; even in private institutions the bureaucracies are similar. The perception is that getting hired (whether or not formal tenure is an option) amounts to "employment for life" and creates an institutional culture structured so that only the most grievous personnel issues are ever addressed. The fear of employee-generated litigation has left many supervisors feeling helpless, despite the fact that many everyday problems may have simple solutions. Organizational rigidity, union rules, and the like may extend or heighten conflicts unnecessarily.

We intend, therefore, to give library managers four basic tools for addressing workplace conflict:

Perspective. We provide background theory, history, observations, and methods for understanding a variety of people and issues that typically arise in the daily work of libraries and demonstrate that these can actually be positive influences.

Methodologies. We offer strategies for working more successfully with all parties involved in a conflict, including yourself.

Examples from real life. We present realistic library scenarios using incidents culled from an informal survey administered over various electronic discussion lists, with analysis from two experts in conflict resolution.

Planning. We provide methods for anticipating and preparing for the management of conflict.

Conflict Management for Libraries was designed to be a practical tool to assist library managers by offering insights on how to identify and interpret the conflicts that inevitably present themselves in the workplace every day. We sincerely hope the book will lead librarians from different types of libraries to examine their management structure and think about the issues we raise. We know we have been influenced by our experience in the academic environment, but we hope that the scenarios and background information will be helpful for all.

ACKNOWLEDGMENTS

MOST OF US PERCEIVE OF BOOKS AS HAVING—AS CULTURAL ICONS HAVE ALWAYS had—the role of conveying knowledge and experience. While writing this book, I realized how writing is also a powerful tool for self-instruction. I have grown as a writer, researcher, and person; however, no one can create a project like this in a vacuum, and I would like to acknowledge those who helped along the way.

First, I would like to thank my coauthor, Eleanor I. Cook, for making this project possible. It was she who was first approached by ALA Editions to propose this book. I deeply appreciate her many contributions to the text and her considerable skill in editing the manuscript. I also wish to thank Pat Wagner and Glenda Hubbard for their willingness to be a part of this venture and for their excellent contributions. Both of them will always have a special place in my heart.

I envisioned *Conflict Management for Libraries* as being different from the standard presentation, with its scholarly insights and statistics. I wanted this examination of organizational conflict to be a vehicle for moving into the very private area of our consciousness, where I believe that most personal and interpersonal conflicts have their roots. I wanted to let people tell their stories and present reality as they experienced it. Therefore, I would also like to thank the more than five hundred people who took the time to answer our online survey for sharing their stories of conflict and successful conflict management with us. This book would not have the depth that it has without their honesty and candor. True to my word, as this book is published, the surveys will be consigned to a bonfire to ensure our promise of confidentiality.

I would like to thank Katina Strauch and the Charleston Conference for being the first professional librarians conference to take the initial "leap of faith" and allow me to present my research on conflict to library organizations. I'd also like to thank the American Library Association's ALCTS and LAMA for allowing Eleanor and me to present on a national level. Both of these organizations began the process that led to the development of *Conflict Management for Libraries*.

I also wish to thank my departmental supervisor, Constance Foster; my dean, Michael Binder; and my colleagues at Western Kentucky University for their patience and support during this process.

Finally, I would like to thank my wife, Lesley, for her incredible patience and willingness to sacrifice her weekends and holidays while I labored away in my office.

JACK G. MONTGOMERY

It took far longer than two years to write this book, especially because I'd never written a book before but also because I held down a full-time job and engaged in other professional and personal activities. I have learned a great deal about many things writing this book. I've learned about procrastination and commitments. I've learned how I can be a better supervisor and deal with conflict. I've become a better editor, writer, and scholar.

Most of the "voice" of this book belongs to Jack. I have contributed along the way, but my biggest contribution has been the editing. I must also thank Pat Wagner and Glenda Hubbard for their substantial contributions. These two consultants have become esteemed colleagues along the way, and Jack and I agree that we are better persons for having the privilege of knowing them.

I also thank my colleagues at Appalachian State University for their patience and support during this process. On a personal note, I thank Glenn Ellen Starr-Stilling for her critical eye with editing and her friendship through the process. To my husband, Joe, my thanks for his patience, love, and knowledge of economics.

Finally, from both of us, thanks to Marlene Chamberlain, Emily Moroni, Patrick Hogan, and all others at ALA Editions who assisted with making this book a reality.

ELEANOR I. COOK

PART ONE

Types of Library Conflict

MOST OF US EMPLOYED IN THE INSTITUTION KNOWN AS A LIBRARY realize that our employer is unique. Although libraries are not usually considered commercial enterprises, they share many features of and similarities to business ventures. Libraries offer products and services, operate on a set budget, have managerial structures, and employ professionally trained people to accomplish goals. It is the management of those people that concerns this study. Within the historical framework of libraries, we clearly see that the institution as well as the professional identity of the librarian is in a period of transition. Libraries are evolving to respond to the demands of the society in which they exist. A natural component of that change is the changing nature of library organizational management.

The American library's organizational heritage, like that of other institutions, developed along certain cultural themes regarding the management of people and organizations. The first was Western civilization's military hierarchical chain of command system. A general conveyed his wishes to his subordinates who in turn expressed those ideas to their subordinates along the chain of command. This was an efficient method as long as the chain of command remained intact. Orders were not to be questioned, only followed to the letter. Every soldier was expected to know and accept his position in the chain of command.

Management as we know it was first "invented" by Frederick W. Taylor (1856–1915), and his principle of what came to be known as "scientific management" was first practiced by the military at the turn of the twentieth century. One of Taylor's concepts was that "mission defines strategy after all, and strategy defines structure . . . differences are mainly in application rather than in principle" (Drucker 1999, 8).

A second major factor influencing the management of institutions was the Industrial Revolution of the nineteenth century, which centralized the workforce in a single location and routinized the structure of the work. Many studies were done in the nineteenth and early twentieth centuries to discover the most efficient method of handling various workflow issues. These early time and motion studies paved the way for the modern-day assembly plant as well as the modern business office. Each aspect of the work was segmented by task and departmentalized. In large industrial settings, no longer did a person perform varied assignments or craft the product from beginning to end. Instead, the worker focused only on one or two aspects of the production. In addition, each part of the administrative operation was segmented by task, leading to the creation of various departments such as accounts payable, receiving, shipping, and so forth. Such departmentalization remains in most businesses and institutions to this day.

During the 1920s and 1930s, managers began to realize that they could not exert total control over the lives of their employees and that people did not work just for money. As businesses became more productive and competitive, managers realized that they needed to find ways to motivate production and inspire some form of loyalty to their institution. With the advent of modern psychology, managers realized that they could and should employ certain methods to retain workers.

Libraries have followed these trends. As Irene B. Hoadley indicates, in the old days, a library director was most likely an unquestioned autocrat, often coming from the upper levels of society with superior education and social status. He (or, infrequently, she) was the central figure of authority to whom librarians deferred on almost every matter. As a result, most librarians saw themselves not as managers but as performers of a service or technical function. Those who were compliant were often promoted. Creative thinking was generally discouraged and self-assertion frowned upon. This attitude still exists in some institutions today, as evidenced by the comments found in the survey of conflict in the workplace we conducted in 2000. Two examples follow: "Every time you express an idea or try to suggest something new, you get punished," and "Our director is an insecure person who is terrified of anyone who expresses an opinion contrary to hers . . . the atmosphere is oppressive."[1]

Although it is impossible to verify these claims, they reflect the perceptions and assumptions of one individual or one group of individuals. That does not, however, invalidate their effect on the workplace. As Peter F. Drucker indicates in *Management Challenges for the 21st Century*, assumptions matter, because what we as managers and employees accept as reality is where we will place our focus. Our perceptions and assumptions "are rarely analyzed, rarely studied, rarely challenged—indeed, rarely made explicit" (1999, 3). Yet the effect on our behavior can and often does constitute our workplace reality.

The exponential growth of universities after World War II and the accompanying growth of libraries as a result of the money that arrived to support those institutions is worth noting. This growth continued until the 1970s when, for a variety of social and economic reasons, popular public support of higher education and consequently libraries began to wane. Until that time, writings reflected a blindness to the idea of the library as a businesslike organization. Universities tended to see themselves as above the idea of businesses and instead were Socratic lyceums where academic credentials magically conferred the ability to manage all other aspects of the life of the university.

This simplistic characterization of library administration is not meant to be a statement of fact but rather one of assumption. As we recall from Drucker, however, assumptions often have a way of creating reality. Numerous comments from our survey gave us the clear impression that at least in some sectors of our profession, the old autocratic perceptions and paradigms persist to this day. For instance, one respondent told us, "They [the administration] see us [the employees] as servants and peons to be routinely treated like dirt."[2] Another early assumption was that librarians and their staff enjoyed a somewhat protected status and a limited accountability for the quality and results of their work and actions. Libraries still are not separate economic units and therefore not full partners in the university or organization. Like a dependent child, the library has needs to be fulfilled but no clearly defined system of production and accountability. Its mission may seem vague, and thus its strategies and resulting structure reflect this organizational vagueness. Our leaders were, in the past, chosen for their academic credentials rather than for any demonstrated knowledge of or ability to manage people or organizations. Society in turn recognized the library's inherent value and supported such a structure. Many of the prevailing concepts of management focused on the reactive control of what already existed, allowing change and direction to come from the outside. Consequently, librarians have also labored under the perception that their technological prowess is their most marketable asset. Instead of focusing on effective management and organizational development of our institutions, we have allowed the high-tech market to drive our organizational response and often our budgets. As Drucker points out, however, technologies are limitations and, hence, cannot be the basis for development of managerial policies

(1999, 29). All of these assumptions have contributed to the situations and institutional climate we have inherited in our professional lives.

We have seen over the past several decades that many of our old assumptions about libraries are counterproductive to our survival as institutions. As society in general is demanding more accountability and productivity from its educational and public institutions, libraries have had to respond accordingly. "The center of a modern society, economy and community is not technology. It is not information. It is not productivity. It is the managed institution as the organ of society to produce results. . . . Management's concern and management's responsibility are everything that affects the institution and its results—whether inside or outside, whether under the institution's control or totally beyond it" (Drucker 1999, 39–40).

This book cannot deal solely with the resolution of conflict in libraries. It must also offer ideas for a holistic approach to the managerial issues that often present themselves as conflict. Our aim is to provide the reader with a clearer sense of mission, so that appropriate strategies may be developed in libraries. Implementing such strategies should have a positive, rippling effect throughout our organizations. Conflict is an inevitable and yet desirable part of organizational life. In the next chapter, we examine the causes and manifestations of conflict in libraries.

NOTES

1. Survey respondent 155, academic library support staff, June 5, 2000.
2. Survey respondent 242, academic librarian, June 6, 2000; survey respondent 321, academic librarian, June 6, 2000.

1

Bringing Personal Baggage to Work

HAVE YOU EVER CONSIDERED ALL THAT YOU BRING TO THE WORKPLACE EACH day other than your briefcase and lunch bag? Every morning, each of us brings to work an incredible package of abilities, education, work and life experiences, physical attributes and shortcomings, agendas, motivations, patterns of behavior, and hopes and dreams. All of this is shaped over a lifetime by many influences, some not so obvious. We bring to work our abilities in how we handle stress, react to change, deal with criticism, work with others, and so forth. We do all this without ever really being conscious of how we cope, what methods we employ, or why. However, these abilities or disabilities profoundly shape how productive our day will be and how we influence those who work around us. In the final analysis, these skills will most likely determine whether or not we will be successful in the overall goals and objectives we pursue in our careers.

Where do these influences originate? What triggers the negative reactions and their subsequent impact? Why should supervisors even concern themselves with such matters? Most people know how to behave and interact at work, we assume. It's understood that employees are not supposed to bring their emotions and personal concerns to work; everyone knows this—or do they?

If the above assumptions were reality, then our libraries would be serene, peaceful havens from the outside turmoil of the world, with only minor disruptions in the gentle ebb and flow of the fabric of daily life. We often find library managers and staff clinging blindly to such notions, often trying to force the square peg of reality into the round hole of such a fantasy. The reality is that libraries as workplaces are multilayered, complex microcosms within larger institutional settings. Even at the departmental level, social structures are profoundly apparent, and everyone has a role to play. So many times the comment is made, "We're just like a family around here." Such a statement rings true more than we know. To try to understand interpersonal and group dynamics, we need, as supervisors and managers, to recognize behaviors for what they are and respond appropriately.

Psychotherapist, business consultant, and author Brian DesRoches indicates that organizations in many ways are a reflection of family systems. He states, "We acknowledge the existence of emotional systems in families, but often ignore emotional realities in the workplace. We act as if people don't have feelings and emotional interactions once they walk through the doors at work, as if these feelings and interactions don't affect the way they do their jobs" (1995, xii).

Most of us have since birth been immersed in a variety of social systems. The first system we encounter is usually the biological, or family of origin. This social system, in turn, is a subsystem of larger groupings such as ethnic or other connected communities based on a common theme. These then are linked to a larger geographic system, then to the world as a whole. Like a pebble cast into a pond, events and developments affect the entire system in all directions. In short, no one grows and learns in a vacuum, biologically or socially, so studying the individual in a vacuum is also pointless. This is the premise behind the therapeutic discipline known as family systems therapy. This method seeks to understand people as interconnected entities within the social systems that shape and mold both the individual and the group in an ongoing cycle of effects. It analyzes the nature and structure of communication within those systems as well as how that communication moves within and is interpreted by those involved. Raphael J. Becvar and Dorothy S. Becvar, in their book, *Systems Theory and Family Therapy: A Primer* (1982), define three basic principles regarding the communication of information in a family system:

> "One cannot not behave. We do not have the choice of doing nothing so long as we live" (13). Our world is like an aquarium; every movement and introduction of something new, no matter how small, affects everything in the tank. The water and the fish are always moving.

> "One cannot not communicate" (13). Even silence sends a discernible message. Anyone who has experienced the "silent treatment" knows something is being communicated, and such communication can be fraught with misunderstanding.

"The meaning of a given behavior is not the 'true' meaning of the behavior; it is, however, that individual's personal truth" (13–14). Studies of witness perceptions during legal proceedings indicate that people take in stimulus of one form or another and process it through their psychological filters based on experiences, backgrounds, and beliefs, assigning meaning to that stimulus accordingly. The meanings assigned to those events can vary widely according to interpretation. And the meaning assigned to the event or behavior remains "true" for that witness until he or she learns of new information about the situation. For example, a person walks into a dimly lit barn, seeing what appears to be a snake lying on the floor. A barn is a likely environment for a snake, but the person may have a fear of snakes or, having grown up in an urban environment, may have preconceived ideas about what might be found in a barn. By assigning meaning to this event, based on prior experiences, the person may deem it wise to remove him- or herself from that environment quickly. Later, the area is illuminated and another common item found in barns, a rope, is discovered to be the actual object. This scenario could be reversed, of course; if someone with limited knowledge of barns walked in on a real snake, thinking it was a rope, another set of consequences would occur.

DesRoches began to notice as he worked as a business consultant that the principles of family systems therapy were being replicated in the workplace. He found that "organizations function just like families, and that applying the systems approach to the problems and challenges of work relationships can be just as effective as it is with families" (1995, xii). DesRoches sought to move away from the traditional approach of identifying the person or persons causing the problem and correcting or punishing their behavior. Rather, he examined the emotional systems present in the work environment and used those systems to help people communicate and work together more effectively. In his book, *Your Boss Is Not Your Mother,* DesRoches describes how as children we learn to function within our family by developing a set of behaviors that allow us to navigate through the relationships within the unit. This includes coping mechanisms for periods of stress when family members are challenged or threatened. From this adaptive learning process, we internalize these behavior patterns as permanent ways for dealing with similar events outside the family circle. Most of us spend more waking hours per day at work than with family members at home, at least during the workweek. With this in mind, it is no wonder that we naturally fall into familial patterns where we spend the majority of our productive time. When trouble develops and tensions mount, we automatically revert to familiar methodologies for handling the emotions invoked. For example, a middle-aged woman with two children of her own works in an office where one of her responsibilities is to maintain certain critical files and records. Her supervisor discovers that she has defied established procedures for retention of these files; as a result, some important records have been lost. The supervisor asks to see the employee in his office about the incident and is amazed to see a grown woman become defensive, begin to cry, and exclaim, "You never like anything I do!" When confronted with the potential for criticism, this person reverted to the posture and manner of a scolded child.

As the above example illustrates, we bring our own private coping mechanisms and expectations of how others will react to those behaviors with us to the workplace. A verbal attack used by one person may solicit a fight-or-flight reaction from another person and is a common behavior used to gain control over a given situation. Most people, without thinking, will enter the fray, taking up the challenge or retreating from the situation. The abusive person has learned at some time in his or her life to successfully employ this approach to dominate and intimidate others or defend him- or herself.

People who engage regularly in verbal attacks generally struggle with self-esteem issues. They then take out their frustrations on those around them. Managers who use this tactic repeatedly create anxiety and fear in the workplace. Generally speaking, fear is not a predictable motivator for success, except under the most restrictive circumstances. "As fear accumulates in an organization, the commitment, motivation, confidence, and imagination of individuals are surely diminished" (Ryan and Oestreich 1991, 70).

Other types of verbal cues include what Robert Bacal, of Work911/ Bacal & Associates, calls "hostile bait" (1998, 1). Such cues may be unspoken or presupposed and indirectly suggest some failing of the person being attacked. In the family, the bait might be, "If you were a good son [husband, etc.], you would . . . ," and in the workplace that becomes, "If you were any kind of supervisor [cataloger, reference librarian, etc.], you would. . . ."

To derail this sort of negative encounter, one must be self-aware, recognize the signs, and work carefully to turn the communication around to a positive direction. This takes practice and skill.

A useful primer that provides assistance with developing these skills is a popular book entitled *The Gentle Art of Verbal Self-Defense,* by Suzette Haden Elgin (1980). It's been around for years but still has great value for situations where you need tools to defuse a supervisor or coworker who wishes to draw you into verbal conflicts on a constant basis. It also is helpful with family members who seem to enjoy replaying certain encounters over and over. Elgin has written an array of related publications that address verbal-abuse situations in different circumstances and with different audiences in mind.

Not all interpersonal skills learned in the family environment are negative—far from it. Depending on one's experiences, extremely useful and constructive habits of interaction can be learned and practiced. However, those that become habitual are often internalized in such a way that if they are negative, changing those patterns can be extremely difficult, especially in times of stress.

Other types of emotional baggage that people bring to work include religious convictions and customs, grief and personal loss situations, and post-traumatic stress disorders caused by past or current abuse, accidents, or other types of trauma. "It is estimated that 25% of workplace problems such as absenteeism, lower productivity, turnover and excessive use of medical benefits are due to family violence" (Employee Assistance Providers/MN). Although many institutions have established counseling centers or access to outside outlets for assisting employees in dealing with such issues, it can still be an awkward and time-consuming process to address these kinds of problems from a supervisory standpoint. Often it takes months or years for overt symptoms to come to light or reach a point where the issue must be addressed in the workplace. The analogy of the busy intersection that needs a stoplight but has one installed only after a tragic accident occurs seems relevant. So often a situation has to reach a crisis stage before conventional office protocols or policies will allow supervisors to intervene.

Further, supervisors rarely have the training to address serious conditions, such as post-traumatic stress disorder or clinical depression. These situations require a professional diagnosis. However, supervisors should be familiar with the general criteria used to define common emotional disorders and should encourage employees to seek help through appropriate channels. Managers cannot and should not approach employee behavioral problems from the standpoint of a clinician, but we must also not ignore behaviors that disrupt and sabotage an entire work group if left unaddressed. Substance abuse, for example, is one problematic area for supervisors. It can be hidden for a long time, but if a person with decision-making responsibilities stops making them, stops producing, or is high or drunk on the job, steps must be taken to let the person know that the behavior must change or the person's job is in jeopardy.

We offer family systems theory here as an introduction to the world of workplace conflict. Managers in libraries large and small and of all types should find these observations relevant. A discussion group (Acquisitions Administrators Discussion Group—Acquisitions Section, Association for Library Collections & Technical Services) at the American Library Association Midwinter Conference in 1998 had a lively session centered around the concepts found in *Your Boss Is Not Your Mother*, which partially lead to the proposal for this book.

In upcoming chapters, a number of other approaches dealing with workplace conflict are explored to complement this one, with the hope that readers will find something useful to apply to their own situations.

Identifying the Actors: All the World's a Stage . . .

THE "DRAMA" WE FIND OURSELVES IN EVERY DAY AT WORK VARIES SOMEWHAT with the type of library in which we work. These variations may be significant, although for the purposes of discussing conflict management generally, they are secondary. The introduction to this book laid the groundwork for this understanding, and as such, we address such variations later within the context of real-life scenarios.

What is more important for consideration in this chapter is the concept of role-playing. Each of us has a role to play in our work environment, and these roles often are similar to those we participate in with our families. According to Norwegian researcher Paul Moxnes, "The family is the first and original organization, not only for man but for most other mammals as well" (1999, 1428). Note that we recognize that not everyone grows up in the all-American nuclear family; whatever constitutes one's "family" can be vastly diverse.

If we accept this, it is useful for staff and management in a library setting to use this knowledge to enhance working relationships. There have been dozens of useful general management works that address how family roles affect how we operate at work. As mentioned in the first chapter, Brian DesRoches's *Your Boss Is Not Your Mother* addresses the topic comprehensively and, in fact, was one of the texts that inspired the writing of this book.

Libraries are a great deal like families because their structures have been traditionally hierarchical in the past. Even though the concept of "teams" has been introduced in recent years, these constructs also have familylike characteristics. Employees serve in a number of roles that complement the family ideology. Library directors, for instance, serve as the patriarch or the matriarch; department heads or team leaders are the "big" brothers or sisters; there are sibling rivalries; there are the "babies"; and there are countless other archetypal relationships that can be derived from a number of research models.

The team model is particularly popular in libraries today, and the roles that come with it are easily ascribed to not only family models but also to sports models. A supervisor may serve more as "coach" than as the "boss," and the employees are judged not only on their specific job skills but also on whether or not they are good "team players." We talk about "ground rules" for communication within a team, and the responsibilities support staff and librarians carry can be similar to players in a number of games. Since sport metaphors tend to be male identified, but libraries tend to be dominated by female employees, most of the game theory is focused on co-operation, not competition.

IF YOU'RE GONNA PLAY THE GAME, YOU GOTTA KNOW THE RULES

There was a group of library employees from a university who would go to a local park on Sunday afternoons to play volleyball. The purpose was just to get together and have a little exercise and some fun; they weren't interested in anything more than that. Some folks from the university's English department also had the same idea. One Sunday the library staff showed up, and English department people were already there. At first the librarians were indignant because the other group had arrived to use the court first, but after some discussion it was decided there was plenty of room for all of them to play. Initially the library played against the English department, but after a while they got to know each other, and they just blended together. Some people drifted away for whatever reason, others came along, and soon there was a core group of diehards that showed up on Sundays. Someone suggested that maybe they should join the community intramural league.

Their experience with the community league was eye-opening. They found out—surprise!—they didn't even know the real rules of volleyball. They'd been playing like a team but without any discipline or rules. Although they thought they were pretty good for a Sunday afternoon bunch, the group found out the hard way that "real" volleyball is something else altogether. One of the better teams in the league held practice clinics and showed them how it was done right. So, with some practice, they got to be "real" volleyball players. Although they never won first place, they came in second at least once and found out what teamwork was really about. And guess what: it took *work*. The Sunday afternoon pickup games were fun, but they were social. Introduce some competition and a passion to do better, and voilà, you've got a team with a goal.

In some libraries where the team concept is introduced, teams never get beyond the Sunday afternoon social stage. This is because there is little follow-through. Maybe they hold a couple of workshops on team building, but do the lessons stick? How much real practice do staff have with the concepts of dialogue, mediation, trust building, and commitment? To be a real team, you have to embrace the rules of the game and live them every day.

NEANDERTHALS, DRAGONS, DINOSAURS, AND VAMPIRES: ROLE-PLAYING DOESN'T ALWAYS WORK

Besides family and sports analogies, a number of popular treatises assign mythical imagery to the roles we play in the workplace. The character labels are meant to fix archetypes in our minds so that we may safely navigate through troubled waters. However, if we allow ourselves to stereotype our coworkers, forcing them into neat categories with the assumption that this will solve all our problems, we often set ourselves up for unintended consequences.

Our coworkers are not mythical creatures. The metaphors utilized by self-help books addressing relationships with "difficult" people do not always seem relevant to those of us who work in libraries. Jungle fighters, warriors, and dragons are not the kinds of people we generally interact with, unless, perhaps, we are working in a corporate setting. That doesn't mean we don't feel this way sometimes about our supervisors and coworkers—no matter what the context, ugly creatures can be found. Sometimes the people who fit these roles are found outside the library itself. For instance, public libraries are often controlled by highly politicized boards or municipal hierarchies that have their own cast of characters.

The point is to acknowledge that labels and symbols are powerful and can be either useful or destructive. Although in this book we reference sources that use these devices, we are not going to set up our own artificial set of labels to discuss how to handle conflict in libraries. We will not call employees close to retirement "dinosaurs" or "dead wood," or emotionally needy individuals "vampires." Others have done this for us. You may find these sources useful or not—just be aware that they can be traps and may hurt more than help.

ACTING LIKE AN ADULT

As simple as the concept may sound, acting like an adult can be a real challenge for some of us at times. Julie Todaro introduces this idea in an article published in *Library Administration and Management*. She begins by observing that "people . . . wanted to talk about . . . the same issue, over and over again, in a number of different states and in all types of libraries. What is this single issue? Employees who can't get along with each other and thus create a problem employee situation" (Todaro 1999, 15).

Todaro's basic solution is that we define for our work groups a set of "reasonable expectations" and "establish basic standards or norms for behavior" (16). By making an effort to talk openly about the way we interact, we gain a greater insight to the range of expectations within the group, and as a result, individuals can better respect their coworkers' needs.

For example, a library's Technical Services team participated in a series of workshops that attempted to accomplish this very goal. Team members discovered that they highly valued common courtesies, such as others saying "Good morning," as much as anything else. They also acknowledged that their particularly cramped quarters and lack of private space for staff (they work in cubicles or open areas, while the librarians have offices) have a real psychological effect on how they get along with each other and with outsiders who come through their space. Another extremely important issue was respect; librarians, especially in higher education settings, are often considered faculty, which creates a gulf in job expectations, pay, status, and leave time. Support staff in academic libraries are often highly educated, sometimes even more so than their supervisors and other librarians. Yet there seems to be a universal complaint from them that they "get no respect."

REWARDS AND RECOGNITION

It's necessary in these times of economic and organizational uncertainty that library managers remember to recognize and reward support staff. As our work changes and transforms itself over and over, we need to not take for granted what effect this constant shifting does to our colleagues' sense of worth and comfort level at work. Staying aware of what is really happening around us is important. If a big change occurs, it helps to celebrate it in some fashion, even if the change is not perceived as necessarily positive. For example, a cataloging department threw an "RIP" (rest in peace) party for their old OCLC terminals when the equipment became obsolete and was to be sent to the surplus warehouse. These machines had been part of daily work life for many years, and even though everyone was looking forward to faster, more efficient equipment, these terminals were the first computers many of the catalogers had ever used, and they had a certain fondness for them. Along with cardboard tombstones and other silly decorations, the catalogers invited the library systems head to the party and asked him to read a few somber verses over the old terminals as a mock funeral. This ritualizing of what was, in reality, simply an equipment upgrade helped the catalogers "grieve" the passing of something familiar and prepare for the new situation. Paying homage to the old machines acknowledged their longevity and their importance to the department's history.

New employees come into our work environments with different sets of expectations than those of our coworkers of many years. Not having a sense of "corporate history," they may not immediately buy into events that everyone else thinks are normal and expected. Managers need to be aware that they may have to assist with and support adjusting the group dynamic to accommodate different styles. When a project is complete or a major goal accomplished, a special box of chocolates may be enough thank-you for someone who has been with the team for twenty years, as it is likely that there is an accumulated understanding built up relative to the specific achievement. If you know this person has a weakness for chocolate-covered macadamia nuts, then the gesture will be accepted as it was intended. However, with new employees, it may take time to find out what works best. A vegan employee won't be able to eat the luscious cream cheese and bacon and egg squares served at the end-of-fiscal-year celebratory brunch— and the diabetic employee can't really feel your appreciation if you give everyone a festive baggie of homemade toffee on Valentine's Day. Similarly, some new colleagues may find most group activities panic-attack inducing, not pleasant. Managers used to lunching together or hanging out at happy hour regularly may find a new colleague hesitant to join in if he or she is battling weight or alcohol problems. Holiday parties can be torture for individuals who observe a religion differing from the majority. A seemingly fun display case idea was developed one summer where everyone in the library brought snapshots of themselves at an early age, and we had to guess who was who. This backfired when it became embarrassingly apparent that our one (and only) African American librarian could not realistically participate. (The element of guesswork would be obviously missing.) However, this librarian took it in stride and kept her sense of humor, but many of us were made aware of how some activities that seem festive to us may actually make some people feel more separate.

Sometimes rituals run their course, and it's time to try something different. In one library, the end-of-the-year writing of the annual report culminated in an all-staff meeting where each department gave a presentation that celebrated their achievements. This event developed into a competition to see who could come up with the most clever and creative skit. Teams developed a *Jeopardy!* game, a *Weakest Link* game, video presentations based on popular movies, rap parodies, poetry readings, and a PowerPoint presentation with pop song snippets. They outdid themselves and entertained everyone. But there was a point where life became so busy and overwhelming that they could not bear to do this anymore. So they gave it a rest and went on to something else.

It's also important to remember that rewards and recognition need to be genuine. Don't force employees to attend social functions. Group activities that are tangential to actual work should always be optional and scheduled when people can realistically attend, especially if not during the workday. A generous, open, and truly appreciative workplace will generate a healthy and positive workforce.

PLAYING POLITICS

One of the oldest classical works to discuss role-playing, albeit obliquely, is Niccolò Machiavelli's *The Prince*. Machiavelli was a counsel to rulers of Italy during the Renaissance. Born in 1469, Machiavelli witnessed some of the most amazing turns of history and, indirectly, helped influence them. An excellent little book that covers the life and times of Machiavelli is *Machiavelli in 90 Minutes*, by Paul Strathern. Although it is true that both beloved leaders and despots have used Machiavelli as a guide, his legacy tends to be thought of as malevolent. As Strathern notes, "His political philosophy was not evil *in itself*. It was just extremely realistic" (1998, 5).

It's a fact of life that politics surround us in the workplace. We can say we don't like it, but that doesn't change a thing. So how can we deal with politics in a productive way? And what *are* "politics" anyway?

Politics refers to the administration of government. In libraries, we are quite often part of the government—municipal, state, or federal. Even if we are part of a private organization, we still have administrative duties that serve the larger organization's operations. When people use the word *politics*, they are often talking about who is in control. Issues of control and power are an integral part of politics. And, naturally, these issues include elements of conflict.

Can we enter the political arena and still be fair, humane people? Machiavelli would say no. But we are not talking about that level of competition. We're talking about petty politics within our own workplace, not national party politics. We can still learn, though, from the most ruthless of players.

There is nothing shameful about playing to win, about standing up for what is right, or beating the crooks at their own games. There is nothing wrong with showing your strength when needed. Librarians, however, are not very practiced at such skills. Sometimes being mean is productive and smart. Sometimes being ruthless, calculating, and aggressive not only gets the job done but also makes you a star—and makes your staff stars along with you. But how does this relate to the world of libraries?

Libraries, big and small, have politics and business issues to deal with. This is the cold, honest truth. And where there are money, power, and egos at stake, there are Machiavellian principles to ponder.

There are few, if any, librarians who walk with the giants of industry, the moguls of finance, or the stars of Hollywood. Laura Bush, the Librarian of Congress on occasion, or a few Association of Research Libraries directors may be the exception. And we can all think of some MLS card-carrying vendors and publishers who might qualify too. If we had wanted to be millionaires, we probably wouldn't have gone into librarianship. Although we all know a few librarians who qualify as millionaires, they made their money elsewhere or inherited it, and they are librarians because they love being librarians—they certainly do not do it for the paychecks.

This is not to say that we don't have ambitious individuals among us. But our ambitions tend to run to such glories as aspiring to be president of ALA, or chair of the faculty senate, or chair of the town planning commission. All noble goals, but nothing like the captains of industry's kind of goals. Yet, to succeed in these endeavors, our colleagues must know how to play politics.

So, Machiavellian principles can be useful—you just need to take them in moderation. Try them on and see what fits—not all of them will, but give the ideas a try. Reading the actual works of Machiavelli is fairly challenging. There are, however, a number of contemporary treatises that capture the spirit and lay out his principles effectively. Several of these are worth mentioning as useful reading for library managers looking for guidance in dealing with conflict in the workplace.

The book *What Would Machiavelli Do?* by Stanley Bing, even though it is focused on the hard-edged business world and is blatantly flip at times, is a good read and has some thoughts to ponder. And it's written for the attention level of Generation X, who do not have the patience for thorough histories of ideas; they just want the executive summary. You can read it in an afternoon.

From the introduction, it is clear that this is a book librarians should read. The author states (and this is the subtitle of the book): *The Ends Justify the Meanness.*

Bing talks about being mean a lot in this book, which is bound to turn many people away. But then he says, "Don't like it? Get over it, you sniveling tree hugger. That's the way things are. If you haven't got the stomach for true success, that's all right. Go be a folk singer or a graphic designer or a social worker or some damn thing like that. The world has a need for people like you as well" (2000, xxii).

"Or some damn thing like that," like, maybe—a librarian? What a surprise not to see *librarian* in that passage, frankly. And it's nice to know he thinks the world needs people like us. So OK, we're not going to become masters of the universe as librarians. So what? We can still manage conflict effectively and be nice people. Nice people can read about Machiavelli and use the parts they need:

- Having courage
- Reducing sentimentality
- Not worrying about whether people like you
- Exploiting opportunity
- Being unpredictable
- Having a destiny, a goal, a passion
- Watching out for threats
- Fighting when challenged
- Knowing your enemies
- Knowing your friends

- Thinking big
- Being loyal and generating loyalty in others

All of the above are concepts in Bing's book, along with a few that are totally inappropriate for our context. We don't take over other libraries, for instance. Also, the chapter on productive yelling somehow doesn't make sense in the land of hushers. Not that we don't have colleagues who yell and scream at times. Perhaps finding a way to do this constructively isn't such a bad idea after all.

Another excellent overview of Machiavellian principles for librarians who work in the higher education realm is an article by Daniel Julius, J. Victor Baldridge, and Jeffrey Pfeffer, published in the *Journal of Higher Education*. Entitled "A Memo from Machiavelli," it is addressed to "Presidents, Senior Administrators and Faculty Leaders Who Would Seek Change" (1999, 113). The article is written as though from Machiavelli himself, in a style similar to Machiavelli's own, although with a decidedly modern and occasionally cynical tone.

Managing conflict includes managing change, which is emphasized in this article. It states that "the key to being effective and the ability to make change begins first with an accurate assessment of the type of organization in which you work. Secondly, you must appreciate how decisions are made and who, if anyone, implements them" (114).

The article goes on to discuss some of the unique characteristics of academic institutions, for instance, that "they are highly professionalized, client-serving systems," and as "people-processing organizations," they have "extremely ambiguous goals" (114).

The authors, in their Machiavellian guise, then describe the decision-making processes of colleges and universities. They note, among other things, that "conflict is common." They refer to the phenomenon of "decision flowing" rather than decision making, since many decisions that are crafted are never implemented or may be implemented only partially or in a series of circular motions (114–15). They suggest a number of rules for the "Change-Oriented," and among these are rule number four: "Know When to Engage in Conflict" (121). The best nugget about conflict within this section has a universal ring to it: "Don't avoid it, manage it" (121).

Administrators in this environment need to have integrity and be able to build trust. All too often, academic leaders let their followers down by not supporting them in times of conflict. At the same time, colleges and universities are vulnerable to outside pressures.

Accountability is another difficult issue to manage. "Many in academe are not held accountable because much of what we do is not readily measurable (so it is difficult to determine success or failure)" (119). Librarians and other faculty could readily attest to the numerous standing committees that exist on their campuses that never meet and do nothing but exist on paper. Faculty list membership on these committees on their vitae, but what does it really mean?

One of the startling revelations of this article is the notion that change in an academic environment can be derailed easily by lack of attention. One of the authors' excellent suggestions about how to make change happen effectively is the following: "The person who traces the decision flow on through to execution and who fights when issues are distorted is the person who really has power. The truly dedicated partisan who wants to implement change is a tenacious watchdog, monitoring the steps of the decision and calling public attention to lapses in implementation" (128).

Academic libraries are certainly not immune to derailments caused by lack of attention. Library directors appoint task forces to study this or that, accept a report, and then promptly move to some new project, never implementing anything. For example, off-site storage, reclassification from Dewey to Library of Congress classification, outsourcing, and reorganization proposals die a thousand deaths all over library land every day. The amount of make-work that well-meaning but uninspired and powerless librarians devote to these administrative assignments is quite amazing. If a library administrator actually believes that a project is worth doing, then it is imperative that talented, dedicated individuals be appointed to make it happen. Otherwise, a report will be filed and nothing further will ever be heard about the project. Sometimes that is exactly what was intended—but should we be spending our time this way when there are so many new, exciting initiatives that are begging for life? It may be Machiavellian thinking to stop wasting our time on dead-end projects, and some may think this sounds threatening—but we cannot afford as librarians to make-work our way out of a job. We could kill our whole profession if we don't have measurable successes. All areas of librarianship are being pushed to conform to new ways of doing business, of new ways of handling information, and we have to spend our time on what will bring us the most return.

3

The Role of Unions

THIS CHAPTER IS BRIEF FOR SEVERAL REASONS. FOR ONE, THE DISCUSSION OF unions and their relationship to libraries and library workers deserves a whole book to itself. The library literature, frankly, could use a newly updated monograph on this topic. Second, much of what *Conflict Management for Libraries* covers can be applied to both union shops and nonunion shops, though where there are differences in the handling of workplace conflict, we want to make note of it.

It may also strike the reader that we seem ill equipped to discuss union work conditions since we are both currently employed for state university systems where unions are not present. Still, as we considered conflict management issues in libraries, we realized that management-staff interaction might vary depending on the presence or absence of a union.

What kinds of workplace conflict differ if a library is a union shop? Any conflicts surrounding questions of wages, hours worked, benefits, job opportunities, or grievances would be affected by union contracts. These are the most common areas of negotiation in a union environment. Any discussions on these and related topics may have special "rules of engagement" that require managers and employees to have a union representative present.

According to a 1997 survey of 891 libraries conducted by the American Library Association's Office for Research and Statistics, 65.7 percent of libraries reported that none of their employees were covered by any collective bargaining agreement (Lynch 1997, 1). The remaining percentages break down as follows:

9.2 percent	Some support staff
20.3 percent	All support staff

23

12.7 percent   Some professional staff
16.4 percent   All professional staff

(The total comes to more than 100 percent
since respondents were allowed to check
more than one answer.)

Librarians and library support staff may both be represented by collective bargaining, although depending on the type of library they work in, they may be affiliated with different organizations. Librarians who are considered faculty are most likely to belong to the American Association of University Professors (AAUP), whose basic mission is explained as follows: "AAUP's purpose is to advance academic freedom and shared governance, to define fundamental professional values and standards for higher education, and to ensure higher education's contribution to the common good" (AAUP).

AAUP serves the professorate in a number of ways. It may serve as a collective bargaining unit for a local chapter, but it also may simply serve librarians and other faculty as a resource for assistance in the case of individual personnel actions. Librarians who fall under tenure and promotion policies may find membership in AAUP valuable even if the organization is not a strong presence on campus.

In higher education settings, librarians may be considered "full" faculty, or they may be considered professional staff with quasi-faculty status. The differences include the presence or absence of vacations, sick leave, and contracts and inequities in pay scales. At many universities, librarians teach classes, serve on university committees, and work collaboratively with classroom faculty in many settings, yet they serve on a continuing contract basis instead of being eligible for tenure. Classroom faculty are often eligible for summers off, sabbaticals, or special off-campus leaves, but librarians may or may not also have these benefits. University library support staff usually are included with other staff ranks on campus and tend to fall into similar categories with clerical staff from other units in terms of benefits and pay. In many systems, there is a library "series" of job classifications that at least differentiates these positions from other clerical types of jobs. Librarians and library staff alike have work conditions that suffer from inconsistencies from state to state and between different types of libraries. These variations may also affect whether librarians and their support staff colleagues are represented by a union. In some cases, the staff may be part of a clerical union, but the librarians, if not considered full faculty, may not be represented by a faculty union.

Other organizations that provide collective bargaining for library employees and librarians include the following:

American Federation of State, County, and Municipal Employees (AFSCME)

American Federation of Teachers (AFT)

Communications Workers of America (CWA)

National Education Association (NEA)

Service Employees International Union (SEIU)

This list is not meant to be exhaustive, but these organizations have been mentioned frequently in our perusal of the literature.

Our reading on this topic suggests, from many sources, that collective bargaining is generally on the decline in the United States. The current U.S. trend is shifting from manufactured goods to a service economy. Libraries fit neatly into this service sector. Jobs that have traditionally been unionized in the United States are moving to other countries. Unions have also decreased because of an influx of women and young and part-time workers, all of whom are "allegedly" difficult to organize (McConnell and Brue 2002, 431).

In many parts of the country, unions are virtually nonexistent because of "right-to-work" laws. In other regions, however, the union culture is still strong and active. We have library colleagues in California, Oregon, Michigan, and Ohio, just to name a few places, where collective bargaining is an important part of library workplace interaction. Two articles reviewed for this chapter outline the history of union presence in particular areas. Mark W. Weber's "Support Staff Unions in Academic and Public Libraries" addresses conditions in Ohio, and Lothar Spang's article, "Collective Bargaining and Faculty Status," describes union representation of librarians at a research institution.

The formal negotiation structure of collective bargaining may be seen as either a plus or a minus in terms of communication between management and staff. The term *bargaining* often denotes that parties come to the table, each with something in mind to win or lose. Is traditional bargaining a concept we want to embrace? If we approach our workplace conflicts as a series of problem-solving opportunities that will enable us to reduce confrontation tactics and facilitate communication, perhaps not. However, some environments may be so filled with tension that structured bargaining may be the best strategy to keep everyone on an even keel. Just as there are library systems managed quite well or badly without collective bargaining, so too exist unionized environments that run smoothly or in turmoil.

Many librarians may think, "With a mission to connect people with information, taking sides [in union disputes] undermines our credibility as neutral collectors, organizers and disseminators of information on all sides of issues" (Auld 2002, 135). During the Marriott strike at the American Library Association Annual Conference in 2001, librarians were challenged to cross the picket lines to attend meetings at that hotel. This was a moment in history when librarians were forced to think about how worker rights in other industries affected their own seemingly comfortable conditions.

There have also been a number of studies about how librarians, like other professionals, are sometimes torn between their allegiance to their professional organization(s) and their loyalty to their unions or bargaining units. Articles by Rajinder Garcha and John C. Phillips, Tina Maragou Hovekamp, and Renee N. Anderson, John D'Amicantonio, and Henry DuBois are a few that address this aspect.

According to *The Employer's Legal Handbook*, "If your business isn't unionized now, it's unlikely that it ever will be" (Steingold 2003, 12/2). Whether this pronouncement rings true in the future may depend on whether working conditions in this country erode or improve. As of this writing, although the United States is regarded as having a high standard of living and a well-treated workforce generally, there are signs that not all is well in every sector. The United States clearly lags behind other industrialized countries in overall benefits and pay for the general employee. Although we have fabulously wealthy entrepreneurs and corporate CEOs, we also have low-wage workers who can barely make ends meet between paychecks and often work multiple jobs. Fortunately, librarians and library workers, though often documented as being underpaid, work in relatively good conditions compared to other industries. Unions may become more prevalent if conditions warrant it. As Campbell R. McConnell and Stanley L. Brue note, "When management treats workers with dignity and respect, workers feel less need to join unions" (2002, 431).

The Specter and Reality of Workplace Violence

OF THE 455 INDIVIDUALS WHO RESPONDED TO THE SURVEY FOR THIS BOOK, 57 reported that their libraries had endured acts of workplace violence. Violence has been and remains a tragic feature of the American library workplace, with no signs of abating. There is a popular myth that suggests that most of the violence in libraries results from some sort of negative contact with the public. The survey we conducted contained numerous statements by directors suggesting that their workplace environment is peaceful and essentially free from any conflicts. However, other survey respondents (often from the same institution) told a very different story. We examine these viewpoints in greater depth later in this chapter, but a look at other literature on workplace violence sheds light on the current state.

The Public Risk Management Association found despite increased security since the September 11, 2001, attacks, violence has not abated in the workplace: "An ongoing study of internal workplace violence revealed that fatal attacks in the workplace have continued at a steady rate despite the renewed sense of security awareness brought about by the response to the terrorist attacks of September 11th. The study focused on violence perpetrated by employees, former employees, clients and other categories of invitees. Since September 11th, 18 separate workplace violence incidents have occurred across the nation resulting in the deaths of 34 people and the wounding of 23" (Join Together Online 2002).

According to the 1999 Workplace Violence Survey conducted by the Society for Human Resource Management (SHRM), 57 percent of human resource professionals reported that a violent incident occurred in their workplace between January 1996 and July 1999 (Join Together Online 1999b).

In a 1996 SHRM survey, 48 percent of human resource professionals had reported violent acts (1999b). The 1999 survey also found that personality conflicts, family or marital problems, and work-related stress were the most common causes of violent acts at work (1999b).

A study entitled "The Experience of Anger at Work: Lessons from the Chronically Angry" found that 11 percent of those questioned blamed the actions of supervisors or managers for their workplace anger. Nine percent responded that unproductive coworkers, tight deadlines, and a heavy workload were the cause for anger. This study also indicated that one in four people were angry at work (Join Together 1999a).

One of the initial inspirations for *Conflict Management for Libraries* came from hearing an account of a workplace shooting by a disgruntled ex-employee in a large urban library. Thus were we motivated not only to attempt to reduce conflict in libraries but also to gain a greater understanding of workplace violence.

What exactly is workplace violence? First of all, it is important not to limit violence to its physical manifestations. Any definition of violence, according to a 1996 *Issues Survey Report* by Pinkerton Security Services, must include "all acts and threats, whether implied or actual, direct or indirect, that cause or could create internal or external stress and physical or psychological harm to employees, their families, friends, property or customers" (Montoya 1997, 18). This definition is particularly valuable in that it recognizes and validates the subtle and long-ranging effects of aggressive behavior, whether physical or mental. To deny the validity of psychological and emotional abuse is to negligently ignore the trauma and destructive consequences of such behaviors, thereby denying the individual's legal right to a nonhostile work environment. In addition, supervisors must abide by "an employer's obligation to do everything that is reasonably necessary to protect the life, safety and health of employees, including . . . the adoption of practices, means, methods, operations, and processes reasonably adequate to create a safe and healthful workplace" (Namie and Namie 2000, 85).

Aside from the obvious tort liability and despite all human resource elements, most employers maintain an organizational posture of denial and subsequent crisis management with regard to violence in the workplace, especially where that violence is of a psychological nature.

Librarians may be particularly vulnerable to and less capable of responding appropriately and effectively to aggressive behavior. We may be prone to tolerating and denying the effects of workplace violence. The problem stems from our professional openness and our organizational culture's service orientation as an ideal. Librarian Barbara Pease, in her article "Workplace Violence in Libraries," states, "Librarians see themselves as helpers rather than as disciplinarians. They have traditionally been unwilling to judge or regulate extensively the personal behavior of library users. Too many rules are said to present a negative image of the library and be a barrier to wide use" (1995, 36). Pease indicates that, with regard to patrons and other members of the outside community, the solution is first to establish standards for behaviors and levels of service and then assert the librarians' right to work in an environment free of hostility and abuse, reminding the profession that "library workers need not abandon their own rights in order to serve the public" (38).

We can apply these same insights and standards to the internal organizational culture of the library. It is clear from our survey that although many library work cultures are productive, nurturing, and effective environments, just as many are not. Pease's theory is that librarians have, as a group, been too tolerant of unconventional, noncollegial, eccentric, and often bizarre personalities within our organizational structure. Our nonjudgmental approach to patrons has evolved into a similar approach to our work colleagues. As long as the eccentricity is harmless, no damage is done. As a profession, we often seem to revel in our individuality. Cultural and regional characteristics may also come into play. Stereotypes regarding certain groups may cloud our thinking when we attempt to approach solutions (for example, Southerners who acknowledge and accept eccentric behavior, as is evident in that region's literature; ethnic groups known for hotheaded behavior; cultural encouragement of repression of emotions, attributed to many groups).

What forms does workplace violence take? SHRM's 1999 survey found that the most common acts of workplace violence were verbal threats (41 percent), pushing and shoving (19 percent), and shootings and stabbings (2 percent) (Join Together Online 1999b). Our survey responses seemed to reflect these national findings when we asked about the specific forms of physical violence:

Physical assault (20)	Other (please specify) (14)
Verbal threats (49)	No answer (122)
Items thrown (27)	

Though verbal threats may not seem serious, many businesses and institutions have learned the hard way to take them seriously as they can often be a prelude to the escalation of violence. Verbal threats may also be used to bully and intimidate others into compliance. In the June 1996 issue of

Getting Results . . . for the Hands-On Manager, supervisors were advised to watch for the following warning signs:

"Threats of revenge against sources of anxiety and frustration" (Violent employees 1996, 6). Examples from our survey include "If I get a bad evaluation from X, I'm going to take it out of his hide" and "If I go down [get fired] my life may be ruined, but hers will be also."[1]

"Ill-controlled physical outbursts such as throwing papers, files, slamming drawers, kicking the trash can, or punching the wall" (Violent employees 1996, 6). An excerpt from our survey illustrates this warning sign: "I came back from lunch, when our head of cataloging came around the corner into acquisitions, screaming that we [the acquisitions staff] were all "f**king morons." She then proceeded to fling a file of papers at us and began repeatedly kicking the cabinets next to the wall. Our supervisor rose from his desk and began speaking to her in a calm voice."[2]

"Attempts to intimidate others by bragging about a weapons collections, marksmanship, martial arts skills, or military service as a sniper, demolitions expert, Green Beret or Navy Seal" (Violent employees 1996, 6).

"Bringing a weapon to the office" (Violent employees 1996, 6). Although it is illegal in most states to bring weapons into the workplace, this can and does happen. This is aptly illustrated by a story from the survey: "I had a coworker who was married to a member of a controversial religious group and over the time since they'd married, he became a staunch and vocal defender of his wife's people's cause. In fairness to her, I never heard her espouse such feelings in private or public, and I think she would have been horrified at her husband's actions, realizing the ramifications of such rhetoric. One day in the office as break time approached, he began to talk negatively about the opposition religious group at the student canteen where we would sometimes go for break. All of a sudden, he produced a small caliber handgun from his coat pocket and exclaimed that he 'would be ready for them.' I began speaking calmly to him, realizing he was in an agitated state, appealing to his common sense. After what seemed like an eternity, he calmed down, and we went on break at a different location for the next few days. When I reported this coworker's actions to the library director, he dismissed my report by saying, 'Well, I'm sure he wouldn't have actually hurt anyone!'"[3] The director's comment illustrates the disturbing trend of ignoring the danger of these types of incidents. Aside from the potential human cost, the legal ramifications of such a neglectful response would be severe.

"Any dramatic change in personality, behavior or performance" (Violent employees 1996, 6). An example from the survey states that before an incident of violence, the perpetrator had "been acting strangely for some time, wouldn't talk to anyone, wouldn't look you in the eye, and was really belligerent when you'd ask him if anything was wrong."[4]

"Openly hostile, or threatening comments about an office supervisor, co-workers, a job assignment or working conditions" (Violent employees 1996, 6). A striking statistic from an article by Larry Chavez, sergeant and member of the Sacramento, California, Police Department and Hostage Negotiations Team, indicates that "incidents of employees killing supervisors have doubled over the last ten [as of 1999] years" (2002, 2).

THE BULLY STILL EXISTS

The concept of bullying, once considered the sole province of the school yard, clearly has moved to the workplace. "Bullying at work," as defined by authors Gary Namie and Ruth Namie, "is the repeated, malicious verbal mistreatment of a target (the recipient) by a harassing bully (the perpetrator) that is driven by the bully's desire to control the target" (2000, 3). Workplace bullying is different from other types of abuse in that it is centered on the abuse of organizational power delegated to the bully. Such behavior is often misunderstood and tolerated as a part of the organizational system of authority. Bullying has never been seriously addressed in the American workplace despite the devastating effects on the individual bullied (most likely to be a female) or the workplace atmosphere, which is poisoned by its presence. Much as domestic abuse was ignored in our culture

for many years, so bullying of adults by adults in the workplace is still unrecognized for the damage it inflicts. Bullying involves the systematic abuse
of people who are organizationally helpless to stop the abuse or fight back
without jeopardizing their positions. Just as on the school yards of our child-
hoods, coworkers will often side with a workplace bully, creating a collective
or group acceptance of the bullying violence. The Namies point out that in
a competitive "winner take all" culture, the bully is often supported, and
the person victimized is further shunned as a loser. They also note that a
collective reluctance to side with or defend the bully's victim is a product of
"Groupthink," a concept George Orwell described in his book *1984*. This
dynamic shields the group from "hearing anything that contradicts their
comfortable view of the world. It's the wall that separates the in-group from
all others. It carries with it a code of silence that plays into the bully's
strategy" (2000, 85). Although individual members of the group will express
concern or regret at the bullying, as a group they will rally around the person
they believe holds the power in the situation. The organizational structure
and chain of authority must be protected at all costs. Standing up against the
empowerment of a bully as a group involves a calculated risk to each
member of the group. What if the bully should select a group member for
targeting and the group turns on that person?

In a social phenomenon called "dissonance," witnesses of bullying incidents also tend to rationalize that the problem is really not as bad as it appears or that it is just between two people (Namie and Namie 2000, 85).
The Namies point out that aside from the consequences to the workplace
environment, often incidents of workplace violence are the culmination of
a long period of workplace bullying. They also note that although the
United States has been slow to recognize this form of abuse, except in the
case of sexual harassment, countries like Great Britain, Australia, Germany,
and Italy are recognizing and in many cases passing laws against such anti-
social and inappropriate behaviors in the workplace (2000, 91–97).

Also, incidents of domestic violence have implications for the workplace. In a 2001 study by Critical Incident Associates of 280 cases of workplace violence, current employees constituted the bulk of the perpetrators
at 43.6 percent, while former employees made up 21.4 percent (Join Together Online 2002). Many of these cases resulted from "domestic violence,
spilling over into the workplace." Domestic violence is not just a private
matter anymore, and many companies are training their supervisors to recognize and respond adequately and appropriately to this social cancer.

WHAT CAN YOU DO AS A MANAGER?

With the problems of workplace violence, the role of the supervisor cannot be understated, yet many of us in libraries have no idea how to proceed. We are ill prepared by our professional education to assume any role regarding the human dynamics of the workplace. Chavez, in his article "Workplace Violence . . . What a CEO Can Do to Reduce the Risk of Workplace Violence," states that an essential rule of the workplace must be to "never, ever allow anyone under your control to strip any person, employee or otherwise, of their personal dignity" (2002, 2–3). He continues: "In many cases, those who have taken hostages or armed and barricaded themselves perceived that they had been stripped of their dignity in some manner. They had nothing to lose by inflicting violence on others. I speak from experience when I say that a person stripped of their dignity is a dangerous person indeed. A person can be hired, supervised, disciplined and even fired with dignity. If you violate the cardinal rule, or allow someone else under your control to do so, you may, in fact, be contributing to unimaginable horror" (2002, 3).

PLANNING AS PREVENTION

The central element for preventing workplace violence involves the old maxim, "An ounce of prevention is worth a pound of cure." Administrators and supervisors must acknowledge that workplace violence is a reality, plan for how they intend to address it, and follow through with the implementation of the plan. The first step takes place during the initial hiring process, including checking references, verifying education credentials and previous work history, and looking for gaps and frequent job changes. In some instances, criminal background checks, credit checks, DMV checks, and drug testing are included. Security consultant Jurg W. Mattman says that "people who have weak job histories, and lots of changes know that employers don't like that and they will drop half the jobs and just extend the time period [for the ones remaining]" (2003, 1). Several respondents to our survey indicated that they had brought a great deal of trouble to the library by neglecting to check references and background. Troubled individuals can present themselves as perfectly normal during the interview only to emerge later as supervisory nightmares.

MENTAL HEALTH AND LEGAL ISSUES

Let us give a word of caution regarding the legal rights of employees with diagnosed mental illness. Although employers are required to make reasonable accommodations for those employees in treatment or under medication, as author Dominic Bencivenga states, this does not extend to allowing a person to become a hazard to self and others. Bencivenga advises employers to first learn about when and how to approach the mentally ill employee when intervention is required (1999, 54). Secondly, there are ways to spot changes in behavior that signal trouble or potential danger. Finally, employers need to know what they can ask of an employee in regard to health information. This is in terms of employees' responsibilities that allow for their protection under the Americans with Disabilities Act (ADA) and also under the recently instituted Health Insurance Portability and Accountability Act (HIPAA). A common example would be to require regular drug tests to ensure that employees are taking their medication or undergoing therapy. HIPAA also requires strict protocol in the sharing of potentially sensitive information in regard to employees' health insurance records (HIPAA). As Bencivenga states, "Although employees with serious medical and mental conditions are protected by the ADA, you still have the right to fire them for valid work-related reasons. If they fail to take their medication, the first time you have to make an accommodation. The second time, that's it" (1999, 54).

FOCUS ON BEHAVIOR

The key is to focus on the employee's behavior and job performance. Attorney Johnnie A. James, in a paper presented to the American Bar Association on this topic, states that the "majority of courts interpreting the ADA have expressly held that an employee's ability to refrain from abusive and threatening conduct toward co-workers is an inherently fundamental function of any employment position" (1997, 5). Referring to *Palmer v. Circuit Court of Cook County, Social Serv. Dept.*, 905 F.Supp. 499, 1995, James states that "an employee who engages in abusive and threatening conduct (whether or not that conduct is related to a recognized mental disability) is unable to perform the fundamental job duties of his position and is therefore not deemed a 'qualified individual' for purposes of the ADA" (1997, 5).

If indeed, as illustrated in our survey, an employee has openly threatened violence, a proper response is to send the employee home to calm down. The key element is to know what to do and when to do it.

Many library organizations found in public libraries as well as those in colleges and universities employ individuals or retain law firms who specialize in handling these types of situations. Institutions often have various counseling centers or employee assistance programs that can and should be consulted in these types of matters. Seeking their counsel is not only prudent but allows the institution to be aware of the developing situation, offering legal protection and assistance to the supervisor should the need arise during the course of the conflict resolution.

DOCUMENTATION AND EMPLOYEE FILES

The critical task for administrators and supervisors is to recognize and plan for such situations before they occur. Management must establish an internal system of reporting and documenting acts of aggression or violence. Aside from the legal implications, most institutional employee policies require such documentation for any employee discipline or dismissal. Great care must be taken in how, when, and by whom the information is created. Improperly created or stored documentation can actually work against you should litigation occur. As attorney Fred Steingold points out, employee files "can be a two-edged sword. They can provide valuable documentation to support a firing, demotion, or other action that's adverse to the employee, but the employee, in turn, can point to indiscreet entries and use them against you. It would be a mistake, for example, to include unsubstantiated criticism of an employee in the file or comments about the employee that are unrelated to job performance and qualifications" (1997, 2–3).

It is also apparent that the types of information maintained on employees can be critical in future relations with that employee. A few other points should be noted concerning the maintenance, security, and access to employee files:

> Make certain the information is accurate. For example, if you write a memo-to-file on an unreported absence or tardiness and discover later that the staff member did call in and you didn't get the message or you forgot to record the initial approval of the absence, you must remember to go back and remove that memo from the file or correct any information that may be incorrect.

Confidentiality is extremely important. Personnel information should be kept secure and available only to those who have a legitimate need to see it. This must also apply to personnel-related information maintained online. The article "The Workplace and the Internet" warns that "employers should never underestimate the expertise of employees in accessing computer information. We have handled cases where employees have secured documents prepared on the company's computer network, including drafts of proposed disciplinary actions against them, merely by accessing the files from their desktop workstations" (Conti 1997, 6). This can and has resulted in employees altering personnel documents for themselves and others. These and other breaches of security should alert the smart manager to look at online records management as an ongoing process.

Software exists that will function like an electronic paper shredder within your system for disposal of e-mailed information. In addition, you need to look toward the formulation of policies and procedures to control how information of a personal and confidential nature is maintained. The article adds, "Plaintiffs' attorneys have learned that computer experts are frequently able to reconstruct deleted documents by examining computer hardware and reconstructing messages long thought deleted" (Conti 1997, 5).

As with all communication regarding personnel issues, but especially with those regarding violence and aggression in the workplace, you need to exercise great care in using electronic media when communicating information of a confidential nature. Privacy with regard to employee-related information must be a matter of the highest priority. Unencrypted e-mail should never be considered private. Use your best judgment as to which storage format offers the most security and control. This segues into one final issue concerning the employee's access to personnel files. A number of states currently have laws allowing employees to examine the contents of their personnel files. Some even allow for documents to be copied, and in some cases, rebuttals to criticisms may be submitted and placed in the file. One way to offer employees a degree of security is to automatically offer them copies of all their employment-related materials, such as job evaluations. Another procedure commonly employed where employees have these rights is to have a third party present as the file is examined to ensure the information is retained and is in its original form.

Be aware that the Americans with Disabilities Act has strict guidelines on how to handle medical information regarding examinations and inquiries, especially when hiring or supervising a person with a disability. For instance, these types of files must be kept in a separate, locked cabinet away from other personnel-related information. The ADA allows for very limited disclosure of medically related information. Many institutions have a person or an office that deals with ADA-related matters; if yours does, it would be wise to check with them and make sure you are in compliance.

Clearly, employee files, personnel information, and records management are not topics to take lightly. Like other types of management, they require careful planning and implementation along with a regular program of maintenance. One final tip would be to establish a single person or group of persons who have central responsibility for the management of this sensitive information as well as a concise policy for its ongoing maintenance.

Once you've dealt with these aspects of documentation and record keeping, you'll need to adopt a formal policy of threat assessment. The legal aspect of threat assessment is covered under the Occupational Safety and Health Act. The act covers workplace violence under its General Duty Clause (section 5a) and "has been interpreted to mean that an employer has an obligation to respond to threats" (Conti 1997, 6). This section covers hostile actions and words as well as sexual harassment.

WORK AS A TEAM: THREAT ASSESSMENT

Author and consultant Dennis L. Johnson believes that institutions should establish a team to handle threat assessment. The team should be "the system a company establishes to receive, investigate and respond to reports of threats," and "it also covers post-incident counseling and debriefing" (1994, 73). Such teams become instrumental in the development of policies and procedures for dealing with employee conflict and violence issues. Threat-assessment teams also perform an educational function in that they instruct employees on the institution's policies on such matters and what an employee's rights and responsibilities are with regard to reporting threatening behaviors. As author Robert Willits states, the threat-management team must "establish a plan so that staff is prepared and knows where to turn if an incident occurs. There is no time for uncertainty when the incident does occur" (1999, 168).

Threat-assessment team members are the individuals who devote themselves to reading and studying the issues in depth. They become a force within the institution that allows for a greater sense of safety and stability among all employees. This is the group that trains supervisory personnel on how to recognize the danger signs in troubled employees and how to act on threats to individual and public safety. Ideally, the team will conduct seminars, educating supervisors to know when and how to intervene. Willits adds, "The overall challenge in threat management is to balance the rights of the individual with the responsibility for the safety and security of all" (1999, 168). We also suggest teaching supervisors the fundamentals of emotional intelligence (discussed more fully in part 3) so that they can more effectively assess and manage their own behaviors and management style.

Should a serious incident occur, a portion of the team conducts an investigation, talks to witnesses, analyzes the circumstances, and collects statements to create a body of documentation. They make recommendations to administration on how to proceed. Finally, the threat-assessment team can help the employees deal with postincident trauma. The value to the institution is that no one is caught off guard, liabilities are minimized, and the employees themselves understand in a clearer fashion what behaviors are expected of them and what consequences follow certain behaviors.

It is critical to stress how vital administrative support is to the efforts of a threat-assessment team. Without involved and adequate support, any such team will falter and ultimately fail, leaving the institution in worse shape than before and the administration appearing negligent and vulnerable.

Supervisors must realize that they set the standards of behavior for their units. They lead by example, and conversely "bad managers tend to infect their departments with bad attitudes. It is like a disease; they (can) spread despair, anger, and depression" (Johnson and Indvik 2001, 459). Time spent training, grooming, and maintaining quality supervisors is like building a fortress against the specter of workplace violence. Though often ignored, both in library science curriculums and in various institutional settings, the

value of serious managerial development programs to librarians' professional lives cannot be overstated. Violence in the workplace is a modern reality, and library managers should not obfuscate their role in its control and
management.

NOTES

1. Survey respondent 22, academic library support staff, June 4, 2000.
2. Survey respondent 144, academic librarian, June 5, 2000.
3. Survey respondent 152, special librarian, June 5, 2000.
4. Survey respondent 331, academic library support staff, June 7, 2000.

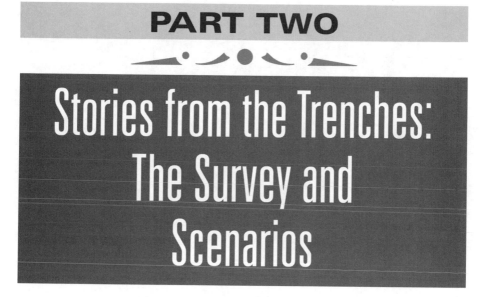

PART TWO

Stories from the Trenches: The Survey and Scenarios

THIS SECTION OF THE BOOK IS ALL ABOUT REAL-LIFE SITUATIONS OF CON-
flict found in today's libraries. The purpose of this section is to illustrate
how common conflict is in libraries and to offer some strategies for dealing
with such situations. The scenarios are composites—that is, none of them
are exactly what happened in any given situation that we heard about in our
research. We hope that by sharing these examples, the reader will realize
that similar situations may be addressed in a similar fashion with hopefully
positive results. We have structured the responses to stimulate the kinds of
questions and issues you should ask yourself when faced with such inci-
dences. Please remember that any actions recommended in the scenarios
should only be taken as educated advice and nothing more. You should always check with your institutional or other available legal counsel as well as
any policies regarding such matters that may be in place in your particular
organization. [*Legal disclaimer:* Supervisors should follow any existing procedures already in place at their institution.]

THE SURVEY AND SCENARIOS

As we began the initial research for this book, we realized that it might be
wise to take a different approach to the management of conflict. We wanted
to do something besides utilizing scientifically based essays that outline the
problem with statistical data. There is certainly nothing wrong with this approach, but we decided to take a more holistic view to the problems related
to interpersonal and organizational conflict in the library workplace. One of
the methods used in conflict resolution in this book requires each person to,
under certain guidelines, tell his or her side of the story and share a personal
view of reality regarding the issues surrounding the conflict. This approach

allows the person attempting to mediate or otherwise resolve the issue to understand how each person views the issue. The subjectivity of each person's view consists, correct or incorrect, fact or fantasy, of how that person is approaching the issues at hand. To deny this viewpoint is to subvert the path to resolution. It is critical, therefore, that people's perceptions be understood and expressed. In short, individuals need to tell their stories, and we need to listen before any measures can be employed toward resolution.

The Survey

To this end we began by creating a survey that would, unlike many surveys that amass numerical information, allow the respondents, in a structured manner, to tell their stories, speak their minds, rant and rave, and otherwise present their views of their reality. The survey was distributed to fifteen library electronic discussion lists during the summer of 2000. The response was overwhelming. We received more than 500 responses from many types of library settings. Of these, 455 were complete enough to use. We received more than a dozen private communications in the form of e-mails and personal letters. Respondents told us both the positive and the negative. Fully one-fourth of the responses were generally positive in tone and comment. This gave us valuable information on what methods and social elements the responders viewed as beneficial to a harmonious workplace as well as those that were deemed negative. We wish to thank all of the respondents for their candor and depth of expression. We have peppered this book with their comments, being very careful to protect the confidential nature of their responses.

It was clear that some people were concerned about protecting their anonymity; some respondents went to great lengths to hide their identities. We received several dozen responses, for example, with e-mail header information blacked out or mailed from some location other than the respondent's residence. We realized that the survey had touched a sensitive nerve in these people's lives, and in spite of the perceived risk, they believed it was important enough to participate. In some cases, heartfelt letters were sent along with the survey, pouring out details of difficulties the respondents were experiencing. We applaud the bravery of these people in taking the time to confide in us for this project. All quotes from surveys have been edited to preserve anonymity.

Another observation about the survey was the inconsistency of some responses. For instance, a respondent might describe the workplace in a positive light, claiming good communication with supervisors and subordinates, adequate managerial support, and a sense of accomplishment in his or her work life. Later in the survey, however, the same respondent would characterize the workplace climate as "hostile," "angry," "paranoid," or "frustrating." The paradoxical quality of these responses reveals the difficulty we have in relaying our feelings about workplace conflicts. Another effect we observed was that we would receive multiple answers to the same question, throwing off the counts.

Furthermore, we often received conflicting reports from the same library, where the director or other administrator would share a vastly different viewpoint than the employees about workplace conditions.

The Scenarios

From these candid anecdotes, we were able to identify common themes and issues that seemed to present themselves over and over in libraries. From these themes, we created seventeen fictional, composite scenarios presented as case studies. None of these scenarios were drawn specifically from any one library, so if the reader seems to recognize an incident from his or her own place of employment, please know that the themes were chosen simply because many libraries experience these same kinds of conflict. All names used are fictional, and any resemblance to any real person, living or dead, is completely unintentional and is totally coincidental. Further, the consultants who responded to the scenarios never saw the raw survey forms and only responded to the fictional scenarios, exactly as they are presented in this book.

The craft of storytelling can convey many nuances and stimulate the human imagination in a manner that strictly factual prose cannot. Everyone loves a story. We tell stories to each other all the time as a method of communication. Historically, storytelling has been an honored tradition in many cultures and is one way of passing on norms and conveying cultural wisdom. Storytelling is a method of passing along information that most of us find accessible. Therefore, we chose to develop these scenarios as our method of presenting the issues that arose from the surveys.

We decided to seek analysis from experts apart from the "library" frame of reference. We solicited responses from two professionals who deal with workplace conflict as a part of their daily responsibilities. One consultant, Pat Wagner, is an "outside" managerial consultant brought into workplace settings to assist with conflict issues. This consultant has no foreknowledge of the specific complexities, culture, or climate. Therefore, she must analyze and develop a response strategy that the employer can then put into place within the context of existing policies and with input from the involved parties. Individuals can then employ these strategies to change behaviors, thus improving the work environment for all. The emphasis is on teaching people how to solve their own conflicts in a healthy, productive, and timely manner.

The second professional chosen to review the scenarios, Glenda Hubbard, is a human relations counselor, an "insider" whose professional skills are employed within an institutional framework and who is a member of the community she serves.

The outside professional consultant has the advantage of being "outside the loop," whereas the inside consultant approaches from an equally advantageous posture when addressing workplace conflict.

Both consultants who participated have extensive experience working with libraries. They were given the scenarios to review and asked to respond as if they were actually going to work with the people involved. To this end we sought the expertise and advice of conflict management professionals Pat Wagner and Glenda Hubbard.

PAT WAGNER

Credentials

Pat Wagner and her partner, Leif Smith, own Pattern Research, Inc., a consulting, research, and training business founded in 1975, which has an emphasis on working with innovators in the public, private, and nonprofit sectors.

Currently, Pat's work focuses on training and consulting with libraries and library organizations on personnel, management, and leadership issues, including conflict management, interdepartmental communication, marketing, project management, strategic planning, change, and community relations. She is a frequent presenter at state, regional, and national conferences, including those held by the American Library Association (ALA), the American Association of Law Libraries (AALL), the Special Libraries Association (SLA), the Medical Library Association (MLA), and the Association for Information Management Professionals (ARMA). She visits dozens of libraries and their staffs each year, from state libraries to special libraries with one employee, from urban library systems to rural libraries in communities of less than one thousand, from trustees and school boards to support staff and volunteers. She has worked with library staff from all types of libraries and organizations: academic, public, school, special, and state as well as library associations.

Much of Pat's work is educational. She also facilitates communication sessions among library staff and provides one-on-one coaching. As of this writing, she has worked with library communities in more than thirty-eight states, beginning with programs for the special library community in the late 1970s.

Pat's Statement of Approach for This Book

Two principles guided my responses. First, conflict can be healthy or unhealthy. And second, unhealthy conflict, particularly if it is more than the occasional human mistake, is almost always a symptom of management problems in the library.

My first job in conflict management is to help move people from unhealthy to healthy ways of thinking and behaving. Healthy workplace conflict is rational. It is constructive, curious about the other persons' points of view, and focused on the present and future, and it seeks to uncover facts and improve both relationships and productivity. Unhealthy conflict, on the other hand, is charged with negative emotion, usually way out of proportion with the seriousness of the issue. People in the grip of unhealthy conflict often seek to blame and punish others. They focus on the past, indulge in personal attacks, and instead of seeking greater truths, spend their time defending their position.

I also help the library staff, management, and leadership create a healthier environment. This can include everything from how to write and enforce personnel policies and how the director is evaluated to ensuring that all staff members, including everyone from tenured faculty to part-time pages, understand the spirit and letter of civil behavior.

The ideal conflict management environment starts with the recruitment process—it applies to everyone! Following is a brief outline of some practices that help promote a healthy work environment. When these guidelines are ignored, they can lead to hurtful behaviors later:

Job descriptions include civil behavior and interpersonal skills.

Applicants are interviewed for interpersonal skills. "How do you handle conflict? Here are some scenarios—tell us what you would do."

New hires are on probation, assigned a mentor to meet on a weekly basis, and given specific feedback on behavior as well as productivity.

New hires are provided orientation information on issues such as sexual harassment, workplace behavior, grievance processes, and conflict management.

Twice a year, employees and supervisors meet regarding behavioral improvement contracts.

The appropriate documentation process is taught and used.

Everyone evaluates everyone—employees evaluate bosses, and vice versa.

Everyone is evaluated on civil behavior, not just on productivity.

Everyone receives training on communications and management.

People are promoted based on communication skills and achievement, not on tenure, professional status, or just on technical and professional skills. And managers are promoted based on communication skills, not just on technical skills.

Leaders model good behavior in word and deed.

Policies are enforced for everyone; there are consequences for good and bad behavior for everyone. Bullies are disciplined promptly, whatever their rank.

So, for each of the scenarios developed for this book, the roots of the conflict are not just about each person's individual behavior. Everyone is responsible. Managers need to act based on both policy (rules) and humane standards (civility), not on whim, emotions, or the personalities of the people involved.

GLENDA HUBBARD

Credentials

Glenda Hubbard, PhD, is director of counseling for faculty and staff at Appalachian State University. This position includes coordinating an employee assistance program (EAP). EAPs have developed over the last three decades in industry and educational institutions in response to observations that employees are often ineffective at work because of personal issues such as depression, addictions, anxiety, and family issues. These problems have caused significant employee absenteeism and other work disruptions. EAPs have proved to be cost-effective, reducing lost work time and employee turnover significantly. She also is a professor in the Department of Human Development and Psychological Counseling at ASU. Employed at the university since 1974, she continues to teach graduate courses in counselor education and has served as a counselor in the ASU Counseling Center. As part of her employee assistance work, she conducts workshops for groups of faculty and staff and mediation sessions for individuals in addition to providing psychotherapy for individuals. Over the years, she has served on numerous university and professional committees and participates actively in working with individuals and groups within her department and college and within the university at large. She has conducted several workshops specifically for the university library and has consulted with individual staff and faculty and with groups from the library.

Glenda's Statement of Approach for This Book

As an employee assistance counselor, I deal with both supervisors and supervisees and must be clear on the perspective of each. Therefore, in these scenarios, I examined the feelings of frustration and victimization of each of the characters. I am a strong believer in systems approaches to organizations, and I do not believe in using such terms as *blame* and *victim*, but I must deal with the fact that individuals in conflict strongly believe in the "truth" of such terms. I approached these perspectives in two parts: (1) taking the role of each of the individuals and discussing his or her assumptions and interpretations; and (2) suggesting what the supervisor might do now to improve the situation.

My goal was to encourage the reader to consider all sides of the situation rather than to consider only the administrative aspects. Hopefully, this understanding will help the administrator to make appropriate referrals to employee assistance programs when needed and to make certain that all individuals know that their feelings are understood and will be considered.

SCENARIO 1
The Internal Candidate

Type of Library: Medium-sized, rural public

Area of Library: Public Services

Caleb Billings felt certain when he submitted his application for the position of associate director for Public Services at the Black Bay Public Library System that he was a shoo-in for the job. After all, he had been the head of Circulation Services for five years, had served as both a reference and a systems librarian at his previous post, and—in his own opinion—was an exacting, responsible, and efficient supervisor. In the back of his mind he had doubts about the judgment of the library director, Jack Williams, but he dismissed these worries, knowing that Jack's past practice was to promote from within. The Black Bay Public Library System was in a remote part of the state, and it was difficult to recruit outsiders, though Caleb himself had come from a distant state.

After the required interviews, Caleb was stunned to discover he was not the successful candidate. The new associate director, Cassie Stiles, started several months later, without the knowledge that Billings had been an internal candidate. However, shortly after her arrival, Cassie found out what she was up against.

Jack, the director, made a passing remark to Cassie that "Caleb might not be too forthcoming" when she observed that he seemed to be avoiding her. "He was a candidate for your position," he added, without further elaboration. Cassie, concerned for her future relationship with Caleb, decided she better broach the topic and soon.

Her first attempt was totally rebuffed, in spite of the fact that she tried to engage Caleb sincerely and with some understanding.

"I've been told that you also applied for this position," she began. "I hope that we can work well together in spite of any disappointment you might understandably be feeling."

Caleb glared at Cassie and grunted. They were crazy if they thought he was going to be cooperative. This was the person who had, in his mind, just ruined his whole career. His main goal from this point forward was to make Cassie's life difficult so that she'd leave. Whatever it took, he decided.

Jack's efforts to stay neutral and avoid the conflict only made things worse. His philosophy had always been to ignore trouble and hope that it would just go away. And, of course, it didn't. In spite of the fact that both librarians were competent and contributed to the running of the library's operation, the strained relationship hurt the overall effectiveness of the system and in many subtle—and not so subtle—ways, made life unpleasant.

Caleb's resentment tore the staff apart and made Cassie's life miserable. At every chance Caleb put Cassie down, undermined her authority, sabotaged her projects, and at times was flagrantly insubordinate. Factions within the staff developed as people sought to stand behind whoever was winning the conflict at the moment.

Pat's Assessment

Jack is responsible for informing Cassie of the presence of an internal candidate during the interview or once she accepts the job. She can then be proactive and seek to contact Caleb and meet with him in an attempt to get their relationship started on the right foot. She should acknowledge his sense of loss, frustration, and possible rejection but propose that they work together as professional colleagues. If Caleb rejects this offer, Cassie can then work to keep Jack informed as situations present themselves.

Cassie must exercise her emotional intelligence and make sure she is calm when she talks or interacts with Caleb. Cassie should acknowledge to herself and to Caleb that though she and Caleb may never be on friendly terms, there is an expectation of civil behavior in the workplace, and he will be expected to produce reliable, quality work. Caleb may not respond, or he may resent the meeting, but the ground rules, expectations, and boundaries for the work relationship have been formally established.

As director, Jack could have prevented much of what transpired by being straightforward in his communications with Caleb from the beginning. Jack should have met with Caleb once he had received his application and advised him that seniority would not be a factor in determining who was chosen and provided Caleb with specific feedback on his performance. He should have acknowledged Caleb's many good points as a manager but made clear to him that the search committee was looking for leadership qualities that Caleb had not yet displayed. Jack could have suggested that Caleb pursue further training or education. Above all, once the decision to hire Cassie was made, Jack should have made it clear to Caleb that his cooperation and civility were expected and required and that Jack's administrative support for Cassie would be steadfast and assured.

Caleb may have been unhappy with Jack's assessment of him and the decision to hire Cassie, but he also should understand that any further advancement or consideration for future promotion rests on his being responsible for his own behavior. If he feels that he cannot comply with the expectations placed upon him, he knows that he is responsible for securing another position elsewhere. Either way, he is solely responsible for his behavior and his future.

Glenda's Assessment

PERSPECTIVES

Caleb: I will never understand why I failed to get this job, and there is nothing Jack Williams can do to change my belief. So he might as well give up trying to convince me. Jack should stop trying to be neutral and take a position. I might not like it, but at least I would respect him for doing so. I might appreciate my job more if he gave me a new and creative task that would challenge my considerable abilities and show the other people that he has faith in me despite his failing to give me the job I deserve. Perhaps he could put me in charge of one of the new programs, or he could pay to send me to a training program so that I could serve as expert in implementing it in our library.

Cassie: I am really angry because Jack did not level with me about the situation so that I could have the complete picture before giving up my other job and moving here. Although he has apologized, he continues to stay neutral, and I wish he would simply tell Caleb to get over it! I believe he has failed to exercise proper administrative procedures throughout this process and that he should reprimand Caleb and stop giving him raises in salary. Jack should schedule an appointment with Caleb and me and should lay out the whole thing, apologizing for staying neutral for so long and informing Caleb that he will no longer put up with the negativity. Then Jack should follow through and make sure that Caleb treats me more appropriately. If Caleb doesn't like this, he can leave!

Jack: Perhaps they are both right about my efforts to be neutral. That has always been my style, but I need to consider other approaches. Next time, I'll level with everybody from the beginning. What should I do now? I'll apologize one more time and look for a conference to which I can send Caleb.

I think Cassie is right about a meeting. I'll meet with the two together and discuss the situation and my expectations. I don't agree with Cassie about reducing pay raises for Caleb, however. I will make certain that he carries out his job correctly and evaluate him accordingly. I will be extra careful to give him appropriate feedback on both the positive and negative aspects of his performance. Perhaps I misled him by failing to outline areas where improvement was needed. I'm afraid that I sometimes fail to point out weaknesses and that I unintentionally lead people to believe that their performance is flawless. I need to work on that!

SUGGESTIONS FROM AN EMPLOYEE ASSISTANCE PERSPECTIVE

Jack should accept responsibility for his failure to take appropriate steps to prevent this situation. He should look for other ways to encourage Caleb to find a useful place for himself in the organization, even to the point of funding a training program. But at the same time, he should inform Caleb that he will not tolerate passive-aggressive behavior. He should apologize to Cassie for remaining neutral too long and should inform everybody that he demands cooperation and appropriate behavior from all employees. If Caleb continues in this pattern, Jack should lower his evaluations, reduce or stop his salary increases, and warn him of possible repercussions.

Authors' View

The central factors in this scenario are communication and action. Jack Williams, the library director, should have anticipated that Caleb Billings, as current head of Circulation Services, would have been disappointed in not receiving the promotion to associate director. Before the new person started work, Jack should have brought Caleb in for one, if not several, one-on-one sessions to

> discuss the reasons for not selecting him as associate director. Assuming that these reasons were well considered and based on established criteria, Jack could have provided Caleb with the opportunity to examine his application and credentials in a new light, perhaps outlining what he could do to be considered for future promotions; and

> allow Caleb to express his feelings and reactions to the decision, but also Jack could stress the need for Caleb to provide support to

the new associate director. As Glenda advised, this would be a great time to incorporate Caleb into some new program, thereby giving him a new or enhanced role.

If after all of this Caleb persists in being uncooperative and subversive, Director Williams must step into the situation and act in support of his new hire. Neutrality in this case is a mask for cowardice on the director's part. Caleb must be made aware that his behavior cannot and will not be permitted to continue, and the consequences of his noncompliance must be clearly outlined. These statements must be made with the full intention to follow through with the promised consequences. Caleb must understand that, in the final analysis, he is expected to be cooperative and supportive and that he is responsible for whatever eventually happens to him and his position in the organization.

SCENARIO 2
But She Has Had Such a Hard Life . . .

Type of Library: Small academic library

Area of Library: Technical Services

"This isn't going to be the usual performance review for Judy," Ellen Thomas thought as she collected her notes and prepared for Judy Smith's arrival. Judy had always been such a reliable employee; she turned in her work on time, kept her statistics up-to-date, and got along well with the others. But during the last six months, Judy's performance had taken a nosedive. She was now late with everything though she appeared to be working as hard as ever.

"I've got to find out what's happened," thought Ellen, "because this is so unlike her." Ellen regretted having to reflect these problems on Judy's performance appraisal, but it was unavoidable.

As Judy arrived for her interview, Ellen greeted her and began the appraisal. Judy's gaze dropped to the floor as Ellen raised the issue of timeliness. "I'm doing the best I can!" she exclaimed. "I'm even trying to help Sarah get her reports done as well."

"Sarah?" Ellen stammered, "What does Sarah have to do with this?"

"Sarah's husband left her and the kids, and she's had such a rough time of it that she's been in the bathroom crying almost daily," Judy reported. As the story unfolded, it became apparent that Sarah, one of Judy's coworkers, had come to Judy for help, and Judy, being kindhearted, had agreed to take a significant portion of Sarah's work. Sarah, Ellen had noticed, seemed to spend a lot of time on the telephone and out of the office on one form of leave or another. Ellen knew about Sarah's marital difficulties, but as she seemed to be keeping up with her work, Ellen, as her supervisor, had elected to say nothing. "Is anyone else in the group helping Sarah?" Ellen asked.

"Well, Betsy has been doing some of her serials check-in, and Connie is helping her with her processing, but that's what friends are for, and after all, Sarah's had such a hard life!" Judy exclaimed. "You just don't know—she was abused as a child, lived in poverty most of her life, and now this!" By now, Judy was in tears as Ellen said in her most consoling voice, "I tell you what, let's take a little break for now and meet later this afternoon after lunch. Thank you for being so honest with me; I understand the situation much better now."

"Please don't say anything to Sarah," Judy pleaded. "I promised I wouldn't tell anyone, and I don't want to get her in trouble."

As Judy left the office, Ellen knew that she had a situation that required some action, but what to do and how to approach this emotional issue were the questions.

Pat's Assessment

Supervisors and staff both benefit from attending workshops on a variety of workplace topics; most institutions offer everything from first aid to nutrition therapy. Staff will be more likely to be able to respond effectively to problems that come up in the workplace with such training. If one's library is not part of a larger entity that offers such classes, inexpensive or free offerings are usually available at local community colleges, universities, or municipal centers.

Ellen should not wait for a six-month review before confronting Judy with data about work slippage. A regular system of communication about work performance will make feedback more useful and feel more natural.

Ellen needs to make clear to Judy that covering for coworkers is not appropriate. She might say something like, "Judy, remember that class we attended last month? You and I are not trained therapists or counselors. Our efforts to help people beyond being a friend can backfire or make things worse. Right now, all I know is you are not doing your work, perhaps because you are covering for a coworker. You don't get to make such decisions on your own. If someone needs help, the organization needs to also be part of the solution, because we are the ones footing the bill. There are legal ramifications as well. Your rescuing your friend could end up getting you both fired!"

Judy needs to carefully consider why she felt the need to break Sarah's confidence. In this scenario, Ellen is the supervisor of both Judy and Sarah, but as is often the case, another supervisor could be involved, which would complicate matters. The main point here is that Judy must concentrate on doing her job and stop spending work time on someone else's problems.

Glenda's Assessment

PERSPECTIVES

Judy: I was always the one in my family who took care of all the wounded people around me, and I played that role in the college dorm. When I realized how much Sarah was suffering, I couldn't help doing everything I could to help her. Imagine my surprise when Ellen called me on the carpet for being helpful! I felt shocked and mistreated, and I felt compelled to reveal a confidence. [*Authors' Note: Was she really forced? She brought it up herself and then answered the question asked of her. This comment by Judy reveals her personal view of the events. Regardless of the facts, this statement reveals how she frames the issues and how Judy will respond to future issues on this topic. It may be a rationalization based on her guilt regarding her revelation to Ellen, but it will surely replace the facts in this case.*] I have always taken pride in my ability to help others, and I think Ellen was most unfair in lowering my performance evaluation. Where is her compassion? Where is her admiration for my kindness? She should realize that my helping Sarah provides an indirect benefit for the whole organization because Sarah's work is getting done. Ellen should have been more observant and noticed what was going on before jumping on me!

I wish Ellen would delay my performance evaluation. She could simply give me informal suggestions and save the written part until after we've figured out what to do about Sarah. I really don't think it's fair if this evaluation is allowed to remain in my file. I want Ellen to promise that she won't tell anyone what I told her about Sarah. Perhaps if she took more time to visit with each of the employees, Ellen might find Sarah comfortable enough to confide in her. I wish Ellen would acknowledge my kindness!

Ellen: Perhaps I will acknowledge Judy's efforts and delay her written evaluation, but I must also make sure that she understands the difference between helping and enabling. I'll refer her to the employee assistance program for help in understanding these differences or pay to have her attend a workshop on this topic. I agree with her idea about meeting individually with each employee to see how things are going, and I'll begin with Sarah. I'll give Sarah ample opportunities to share with me her feelings about her life. If she does not do so, I'll ask her specific questions about job duties, and perhaps she'll admit that others are doing some of her work for her. Assuming she admits this, I'll offer her the opportunity for a leave of absence or a reduction in work hours for a few weeks, and I'll refer her to the employee assistance program for additional help. If Sarah does not admit her failure to do some tasks, I'll watch her work more closely to try to find out the truth without breaking Judy's confidence.

SUGGESTIONS FROM AN EMPLOYEE ASSISTANCE PERSPECTIVE

Ellen should acknowledge Judy's efforts and delay her written evaluation but make sure that Judy understands the difference between helping and enabling. She should refer her to the employee assistance program for help in understanding these differences or pay to have her attend a workshop on this topic. In addition, she should meet individually with each employee to see how things are going, beginning with Sarah. If Sarah chooses not to address the problem, Ellen should ask her specific questions about job duties, hoping to elicit an admission that others are doing some of her jobs for her. Assuming she admits this, Ellen should offer her the opportunity for a leave of absence or a reduction in work hours for a few weeks, and she should refer her to the employee assistance program for additional help. If Sarah does not admit her failure to do some tasks, Ellen should watch her work more closely to try to find out the truth without breaking Judy's confidence.

Authors' View

Ellen needs to pay attention to what is going on with staff who report to her, no matter how busy she is with her own responsibilities. Being a supervisor requires day-to-day knowledge of the work environment. Making this effort will go a long way toward nipping problems in the bud before they escalate. No employee should have to wait for a routine performance appraisal to hear concerns about his or her work. Any such concerns should be expressed as soon as they are evident.

Staff with serious personal problems of any kind should be steered toward professional assistance whenever possible. It is neither the supervisor's nor the coworkers' responsibility to intervene in such situations; however, such individuals may be instrumental in encouraging the troubled employee to seek such help. The keys are knowing where to draw the line and making sure not to break confidences whenever possible. Seek legal advice if you think that someone may be endangering him- or herself or others, but do so within the context of your own environment—as we repeatedly wish to emphasize, we are not able to advise on specific scenarios, and it's up to you to decide what is prudent in your particular situation.

SCENARIO 3
It Is Obvious We Do Not Matter

Type of Library: Large university library

Area of Library: Technical Services, Serials Department

Peter Brown hurried from the department heads' meeting back to the Serials Department to share what he had learned and, as he had been instructed, to solicit the input of staff regarding the proposed new departmental restructuring. Recently hired in his position, Peter wanted to make a good impression on his colleagues and administrators by having plenty of staff input for the next meeting. Since he'd arrived, he had tried to communicate with the serials staff about various ideas and procedures he'd envisioned, but he found them strangely uncommunicative and withdrawn to the point of sullenness. "Whatever you want!" they'd reply to his ideas, offering no feedback whatsoever.

"I hope I can get them interested in this program," Peter thought. "I need their advice, but how can I get them to talk?"

Peter announced that he had some exciting news to discuss with his staff and called a meeting in the conference room for 11:00 a.m. The serials staff began to shuffle in, with their usual downcast expressions. "Like prisoners to an execution," Peter thought, "but I've got to try." He began by thanking them for coming and told them he needed their advice and support to make the new program a success. He began to outline the issues as he understood them, to a silent house. After asking for their input twice with no response, he exclaimed, "What is going on here? Don't you want to have any say in how things happen?"

"You don't understand," replied Sheila. the most senior staff member. "You haven't been here long enough!"

"Understand what?" Peter replied. "What is it I don't understand?"

"It's simple," replied Sheila. "For years the librarians have come to us saying they want our opinions, our advice, and our input. We gave them all the cooperation they wanted, gave them advice, wrote reports, and supplied statistics, and what did we get in return? Nothing! Not a thank-you, not an acknowledgment, and none of our ideas were ever implemented. If they were, it was under someone else's name. You'll excuse us if we don't get excited anymore." Sheila looked at the others, and they nodded in agreement. "We're just the staff, and it's obvious we don't matter!"

Peter stood silent for a moment. "I'm sorry," he muttered. "Maybe we can change that. Let's get together at another time."

As they filed out of the room, he thought, "Is all this true?" He had noticed that there appeared to be a social "gap" between the librarians and the staff. This gap was not so uncommon in libraries in his experience, but he had no idea the negativity ran so deep here. Even if the situation was as bad as Sheila had described, what could he do to change the atmosphere and make the department more responsive? He did need their advice and their cooperation to implement the new restructure, but how would he ever get it?

Pat's Assessment

Before coming into a new supervisory position, it is important to find out as much as possible about the library's governance model. If staff seem reluctant to share concerns and show signs of low morale, and if there seems to be a big gap between librarians and staff in general, be sure to ask the following questions of your interviewer:

> In general, do staff get a chance to give input about work processes and changes?
>
> Are people from different departments allowed and encouraged to work together on projects?
>
> Is there any budget for continuing education?

Do the people reporting to supervisors have any say in the hiring
process?

These are just for starters. Get a feel for why there may be discontent,
if you perceive it, and make sure that you express concern about turning
this around once you are on the job as the supervisor (if you decide to accept the position).

Once you are on the job, work on building rapport and developing trust.
Show staff by your actions that something will happen and that positive
change is possible. Depending on how large the operation is, say hello (and
more, if possible) to every employee in your unit, every day.

Remember that old 3/3/3 rule: one-third of the people will love change,
one-third will be indifferent, and one-third will actively resist it and may be
openly hostile. You won't be able to change the past, but you can start on
day one to work toward something better than they have had before.

When a great idea comes up, always give credit where it's due. Remind
people constantly of the big picture so they don't get stuck worrying about
only their little corner of the library. Get staff involved in collecting feedback about services they provide so they can see for themselves where the
problems are. Don't ask them to simply believe something is a problem because *you* (or an administrator) says it is—let them hear it from their
coworkers firsthand.

If you have to say no to something, explain why—and what the cost of saying yes would be, and how it would affect other departments if implemented.

Always share information from above or outside as quickly as possible—
staff will appreciate it when they are not the last to know.

Lastly, always follow up on suggestions—and follow through! Show respect to those who work for you, and in turn, they will come to show you respect. If there is resistance, make sure to treat resisters fairly, and make sure
they have to take responsibility for their concerns.

Glenda's Assessment

PERSPECTIVES

Staff (Sheila and others): We do most of the work around here, but we are
treated like the "hired help," with no respect. The longer we stay, the more
certain we are that when librarians ask for input, they don't really mean it.
They either ignore our ideas or claim that the ideas were their own. So why
bother?

We would like to be treated as important people. We'd like credit for our suggestions, and we'd like to be addressed with respect. We want the librarians to say "good morning!" and look us in the eye when they say it. If Peter wants our opinions, he needs to take time to sit down with each of us individually, noticing what we do and complimenting us on these accomplishments. He might consider having a retreat and pairing up librarians with staff members so that we can get acquainted. It would be nice if he would establish some formal way to recognize our accomplishments.

Peter: I will meet with the librarians who work with the staff to discuss some simple strategies, such as encouraging them to make a point of greeting staff members warmly and showing an interest in them. I have noticed that several of the librarians are so task oriented that they appear to have tunnel vision, not even noticing the staff members nearby. When someone mentions this to them, they respond by saying something like, "I have too much to do," or "I am just an introvert and can't do anything about it." I will enlist their help in planning some kind of recognition program such as "employee of the month," accomplishments on a bulletin board, sending descriptions of people's accomplishments to the institution's employee newsletter, and so forth. Unfortunately, I am aware that this attitude characterizes staff throughout the institution, not just in the library. I will ask the human resources and employee assistance staff to consider offering a workshop institution-wide to deal with this problem. I think the idea of a retreat for library personnel is a good one, and I will bring in an outside facilitator to conduct a team-building experience.

SUGGESTIONS FROM AN EMPLOYEE ASSISTANCE PERSPECTIVE

Peter should schedule a consultation appointment with the director of the employee assistance program and should ask that individual to meet with the employees individually or in small groups to elicit their suggestions. Then he or she should plan a workshop to address these suggestions. If librarians and staff members are paired for some activities, each might be asked to write articles about his or her partner for inclusion in a newsletter or posting on the web page.

A special workshop might be held to encourage librarians to become aware of their obligation to greet staff warmly regardless of their introversion or workload. They need to be reminded that they are paid significantly more than are the staff members and that their obligation to bridge the gap is greater. Other topics of the workshop could include emotional intelligence training, active listening skills, and other methods of showing respect toward others.

Peter should develop a recognition program that includes listing of accomplishments on the web page, bulletin board, newsletter, and other prominent locations, and he should post pictures and articles about each employee.

Authors' View

So often these days, we are so swamped with work that we forget that the people around us are affected by our actions. The interactions we have with our staff and colleagues are very important to the achievement of the overall goals of the library, no matter with which department or unit we are involved. As a supervisor, you set the tone for the group, and if you are new to a group, you can truly make a difference. You can turn around a dejected, demoralized work team. It won't happen overnight; the keys are attentiveness and consistency.

It's important to balance the inflow with the outflow of information. If you spend all your time on outside activities in order to impress your superiors, ignoring the daily operation you are supposed to be running, you will have a great deal of damage control to manage in the long run.

In this scenario, Peter has his work cut out for him, but if he sticks with it and shows himself to be a trustworthy supervisor, he will likely find that the staff will, with time, develop more self-assuredness and pride in their work.

SCENARIO 4
I Don't Have to Listen to This!

Type of Library: Large, urban university library

Area of Library: Technical Services

"What a nice afternoon," Technical Services Chief Don Murray mused as he gazed out the window of his office. His reverie was interrupted when there came a loud knock on his office door. "Come on in," Don said.

It was Janice Smith, a new student worker in the department. Janice was reliable and did satisfactory work. Her hair and clothes were a bit unconventional, but Don made allowances for undergraduate students' dress since they were in Technical Services and out of the public's sight. "I don't have to listen to this stuff!" Janice shouted. "And you'd better do something or I'm going straight to the dean!"

"Please sit down," Don said calmly. "What seems to be the problem?"

"I'll tell you what the problem is; it's Stan Johnson. He won't leave me alone! He keeps telling me I'm going to hell if I don't mend my sinful ways, dress differently, and go to church. I told him I had my own beliefs and that they were none of his business. Now he's leaving Bible tracts in my book bag. I don't have to put up with this to have a student job!"

Don sat back for a moment and thought. Stan Johnson was a good employee who had been in his position for many years. Don knew Stan to be a family man who was very religious and spent many hours outside work in the service of his church. He was also the father of two daughters, which is why Don had assigned Janice to Stan's area. This was Stan's first experience as a supervisor, and Don had no idea that Stan would try to convert or preach to Janice.

"Can I ask you a question?" Don finally replied. "Have you and Mr. Johnson ever discussed religion or religious beliefs during work?"

"When I first started here, we may have talked about it briefly; yes, I think he asked me where I went to church, and did I read the Bible and so forth," said Janice. "But I never said I wanted to be preached at on a daily basis, and now I want it to stop!"

"I understand," said Don. "I'm simply trying to learn how all this got started. If you'll give me some time, I will speak with Mr. Johnson, and we'll see if we can't work something out, OK?"

"Fine," Janice responded. "But if this doesn't stop and soon, I'm telling my parents, and they'll hit the roof!"

"I appreciate your patience," Don replied. "Just give me a few days to do what I need to do."

As Janice left the office, Don wondered how much time he really had to solve what promised to be a very delicate matter. He wondered if he should tell his boss, the library dean, or if he could handle it himself.

Pat's Assessment

To help prevent this kind of incident, Don's library can benefit from management and supervisory training for the staff. With help from the state professional organization and from national organizations including such American

Library Association divisions as the Library Administration and Management Association (LAMA), the Library Support Staff Interest Round Table (LSSIRT), and the Council on Library/Media Technicians (COLT), he can design a program that will help his managers learn good management skills. He may want to bring in peer trainers—such as other librarians and support staff from nearby libraries—who practice and teach the tenets of good management to help instill these tenets in his staff. By establishing long-term goals, over a five-year period, he can work on creating a new culture, which will include the following premises:

> Being a manager is more than just being good at the technical aspects of the job—first and foremost, it means being good with people.
>
> Anyone who wants to obtain or keep a manager's job must go through training and certification, which is open to everyone at the library, even staff without an MLS.
>
> All new managers will be assigned a mentor—an experienced manager who will meet with them once a week during a six-month probation period, in addition to their evaluation and coaching meetings with their supervisors and trainers.

Don's managerial training should include sessions especially for direct student supervisors during which they receive not only information on university rules regarding student/faculty/staff relations but also information about drugs, alcohol abuse, health issues, emotional issues, and current theories in counseling and learning.

The student workers, meanwhile, must have their own training. It is imperative that Don and the other departmental managers include time and money in their modest budgets for actual training of the student staff—not just throwing them into the work with no training or orientation, as is true in many colleges. At the very least the students should receive clearly written information about rules and regulations.

With the Stan and Janice problem, Don may need outside help—the Human Resources Department is an excellent source of information and support. The human resources office representative can outline for Stan what, according to state and federal law, he could and could not do and say in the workplace. It may also help to seek out a Christian minister that Stan trusts to help point out to Stan the importance of obeying the laws of the land—his conversion efforts on Janice are a legal issue, not only a religious one. Don should make it clear to Stan that the rules protect Stan from harassment as well as everyone else. Stan will be welcome to help change the rules, but he cannot disobey them without consequences.

To prevent the situation from escalating, Don should tell Stan firmly, "I don't know what exactly happened, or who was right or wrong. But, in the future, please refrain from discussing your religious beliefs with students on the job. If a student is interested, you are free to invite him or her to your church, but that is all." He should warn Stan that another incident could mean disciplinary action.

To avoid tension in the library, Don can reassign Janice to a different manager.

Glenda's Assessment

PERSPECTIVES

Don: Unfortunately, I did not anticipate the problem, and I failed to train a new supervisor adequately. So, in some ways, I blame myself for this problem, but I also acknowledge that I am not adequately prepared to deal with accusations of restricting free speech or of restricting the practice of religion. I wish that I had worked harder on a training program for new supervisors and had checked out the legal implications of asking an employee not to attempt to proselytize students. I will confer with the university attorney for suggestions about this.

I think my next step is to reassign this student to another supervisor and to discuss with Stan the need to separate his work from his religious practices. I will assure him that I respect his desire to improve the welfare of students but that I must ask him to avoid the subject of religion with them. If he responds positively, I will offer to assign another student to help him if he will avoid the forbidden subject. If he responds negatively, I will ask the university attorney to meet with us to discuss the legal implications. Later, I will schedule supervisor training sessions on various topics each semester and will implement a system of meeting one-on-one with students to ask them to evaluate the supervision they receive.

Janice: I don't think Don is doing his job! He should protect me from religious zealots. This is a state university, and the law says I should not be exposed to religious indoctrination. If Don doesn't get Stan off my back, I'm going to ask my parents to get them both fired!

Stan: As a Christian, I have an obligation to witness to the unsaved wherever they are. Any true Christian would try to reach out to others, and this poor young woman needs the true message of Christ's love. No rule is higher than that!

SUGGESTIONS FROM AN EMPLOYEE ASSISTANCE PERSPECTIVE

Don should consult the university attorney to make certain that he is completely clear on the legal aspects of the situation. He should then speak with Stan, explaining the law. At this point, the situation has become so inflammatory that Janice should be assigned to someone else. If Don decides not to assign another student to Stan, he should give him other responsibilities so that there is no appearance of letting him avoid doing his share of the work.

Before he assigns students to supervisors in the future, he should plan a supervisory workshop with one of the presentations including legal and ethical aspects of supervising students in a state institution.

Authors' View

Assigning the responsibility for supervising student assistants is something that needs to be carefully considered. Not everyone has the knack for managing this class of workers. It is possible for staff and librarians to work successfully with student assistants without actually being their supervisors, and in fact, sometimes that is the best way to handle it. Many times a particular staff person in a unit is assigned the responsibility of hiring, evaluating, managing payroll for, and disciplining student assistants. In the meantime, these student workers may be assigned throughout the unit to work with various staff and librarians who simply coordinate specific tasks on a day-to-day basis. If there are problems, the student is referred back to the supervisor.

In Stan's case, he may have the potential to be a good supervisor of students, but before that is determined, he needs specific training in managerial principles so that he understands the many boundaries that need to be respected in the supervisor-student relationship. Not all students are as assertive as Janice; some would react differently in this situation, and sometimes the reactions would have worse consequences. Don is correct to act immediately; good first steps are transferring Janice to another section or unit (when possible—which it isn't always) and helping Stan realize that his actions are not appropriate in the workplace. It's important to respect people's religious and cultural beliefs, yet boundaries must be set in order for people from different walks of life to work well together.

SCENARIO 5
Love in the Afternoon

Type of Library: Small-town public library
Area of Library: Administration, cross-departmental

Director Bonnie Slagell was just opening her e-mail Thursday morning when her assistant director, Mary Anne Post, appeared in her doorway.

"We need to talk," she stated. "There's something you should know."

Bonnie was disturbed by her tone; though she was hoping for a quiet morning, she asked Mary Anne to come in and sit down. Mary Anne closed the door carefully, indicating the gravity of the business at hand.

"It's about Suzy Cameron and William Bradford," Mary Anne began in a low voice. "They have become, you know, involved."

"No, I didn't know," Bonnie said. "What do you mean by 'involved'?"

With a sigh, Mary Anne blurted, "Bonnie, they're lovers! Last week, one of the staff went into the supply room to get some printer paper and caught them, how do you say it, in the act."

"Good grief!" Bonnie exclaimed. "How long has this been going on? I find this hard to believe!" Bonnie had known Suzy and William for years. They were both fine librarians with excellent credentials, and William was married to the daughter of a prominent citizen, Judge Brown, who was the chair of the library board in their small community.

"As far as I can determine, about six months." Mary Anne added, "They were seen going into a motel together just south of town last May. Several of the staff have come upon them kissing in their offices, and then, of course, there is the incident the other day in the supply room. Bonnie, can you imagine what is going to happen if William's father-in-law, the judge, learns of this? You know he is famous for his temper and vindictive spirit."

Bonnie shook her head slowly. She had worked for years to build a good relationship with the judge and knew that what Mary Anne was saying was true.

"We'll be lucky if we aren't ridden out of town on a rail for allowing this to happen! They will say we allowed a marriage to be destroyed under our very noses!" Mary Anne exclaimed, wringing her hands.

"Let's calm down," Bonnie said. "Maybe the judge won't find out, and the situation will sort itself out. Besides, Mary Anne, what could I possibly say to them? Stop having an affair? I wouldn't even know how to bring up the topic!"

"Do you really think the staff are going to take an oath of silence?" Mary Anne asked sarcastically. "I've worked at this library for fourteen years, and I don't want to lose the only professional job I've ever had. You'd better do something about this situation if you want my support. We are sitting on a public relations powder keg!"

"All right, Mary Anne," Bonnie sighed. "I will look into it right away." As the door closed, Bonnie felt a profound sense of dread settle over what was an otherwise beautiful day. "How could this have happened?" she asked herself. "And just what am I going to do?"

Pat's Assessment

One of the hard issues for Bonnie to deal with, being a small-town library director, is helping her staff and board understand their professional roles. Although many relationships may be built on decades of friendship, she needs to stress that there are limits that must be respected. She and the library board will have to have honest discussions about making public decisions that might be unpopular.

The staff seem to have trouble understanding boundaries and professional discretion. Bonnie will have to privately reprimand her staff for gossiping at the library.

The other issue Bonnie has trouble with is tattletale staff members. She should call a staff meeting to outline what kinds of behavior are appropriate to report and to whom information should be reported. The basic rules should include the following:

> A report to the *supervisor* is proper if a coworker is observed destroying or harming library property, harming another person, stealing from the library or another person, using inappropriate language or behavior with a staff member or the public, or breaking library law regarding privacy, censorship, or the public's access to information or engaging in other illegal, dangerous, or damaging activity.

A report to the *director* is proper if staff members feel they are not getting an answer regarding a problem already reported, or if the problem involves a direct supervisor, or if they want to talk privately about an issue not directly related to work.

A report to the *library board* is proper if staff members feel they are not getting an answer from the director or if the issue involves the director.

A gray area is behavior that might affect how the library is seen in the community or how it affects the morale of the staff. Bonnie should address proper and improper behavior, including cursing, undue sarcasm, appropriate dress, personal grooming, and even seemingly harmless behaviors like chatting with friends at the front desk. Some people regretted the loss of informality, but when Bonnie asked them to imagine how much *they* appreciated the friendly, professional staff at a terrific, high-class store, most everyone picked up on the analogy and perked up. People started to dress up a little more at work and informed their friends that they would meet them to chat at lunch but not at the reference desk.

The state library and some useful websites from other municipalities can help Bonnie, the library board and staff, and the director draft a simple grievance policy so that everyone can weigh in on difficult situations. Several speakers can be brought in—including a police officer, the county attorney, a social worker, and a member of the state library board—to discuss general personnel issues with the staff. The staff need to understand when *reporting* becomes *tattling*. (Telling a supervisor when a coworker is five minutes late from break is tattling; telling a supervisor when a coworker is observed stealing is responsible reporting.)

When Suzy and William's affair is brought to her attention, having policies in place that support a professional environment will make Bonnie's job far easier. The issue is not morality; that is no one's business except the immediate participants. What matters is how their behavior affects the library. When Mary Anne informs Bonnie of the situation, Bonnie should do some discreet checking on her own and act quickly.

Bonnie should call in Suzy and William individually. Her speech should be short and to the point: "I have heard that you are not conducting yourself in a businesslike manner in the library. If I know, probably half the town knows. Do what you want on your own time, but you will behave as polite strangers here. If you don't want to conduct yourself appropriately, you are choosing not to work here. You will both be disciplined equally and fired together. And, off the record, I am suspicious that you are acting out in public, as if you want to get caught. I am furious that you would hurt this library with your choices."

Because the staff are buzzing, Bonnie needs to call in Mary Anne and the other managers, one at a time, and tell them to put a lid on the gossip and to leave the lovebirds alone.

Glenda's Assessment

PERSPECTIVE

Bonnie: I should have noticed earlier, but I am so busy I just don't have time to watch every staff member every minute. It's not my job to be the morals police! The staff expect me to take responsibility for the failure of a marriage. I can't do that! I acknowledge that it is my job to make sure that staff behave professionally while in the building I supervise, but their personal conduct outside of work is their own business. I also cannot take responsibility for whether or not the judge is pleased—he also cannot control the behavior of other adults, even if they are part of his family.

SUGGESTIONS FROM AN EMPLOYEE
ASSISTANCE PERSPECTIVE

Bonnie should call Suzy and William in individually and explain the rules of the building. If either asks for her source of information, she should not reveal the source but make it clear that she will be observing carefully what goes on in the library. She should make no report to the staff or the library board. If any staff member comes to her, she should explain her position and refuse to be coerced into discussing with one staff member the morals of another. She should also explain to the staff that gossip and tattling are not appropriate and will not be tolerated.

Authors' View

Variations on this scenario abound in all workplaces. When the relationship is between a supervisor and a subordinate, there are likely going to be issues regarding sexual harassment should the relationship deteriorate. Follow the guidelines for your institution if you must deal with this situation. When the relationship is between two consenting adults with no other complications, one can only wish them well and remind them to conduct themselves as professionals while on the job. When there are other people affected, such as spouses, children, or other family members, it can become more awkward.

Preaching against immorality directly is never appropriate and usually ineffective; instead, asking employees in such a situation to think about how their choices of action affect others (including their coworkers) is a better strategy. What happens outside the workplace cannot be controlled; what happens during the workday is a different matter. It is likely that an employee in the throes of a new personal relationship (regardless of who is the love interest) may act distracted, show new, sudden absentee patterns, or other symptoms resulting from being love-struck. If the relationship is a hidden affair rather than a normal courtship, such symptoms may be intensified. If the behavior gets out of hand, as in this case, disciplinary action may be warranted, although most people can control themselves and don't carry it that far. Often times a breakup is the worst period to endure (not only for the couple, but for everyone around them).

Supervisors may not hear directly about such developments, but the grapevine always does. Use it when necessary—pretending it doesn't exist only will make you the last to know! And while you may wish to advise employees that it's never a good idea to date a coworker, in many cases the only way to convince someone of this is for it to happen to them. If the relationship sours, the individuals still have to work together. Clandestine relationships gone bad can wreck one's good standing, cost someone a job, and bring misery to innocent family members. Is it worth it? Such distraction to the social environment of the workplace is often quite destructive. Occasionally we do find our true soul mate at work—and if this happens, professionals make sure that they separate their personal lives from their work lives as soon as they determine it's the "real thing." Otherwise, the situation can get too close for comfort. Furthermore, it is important to remind employees that if they enter into relationships with coworkers where the potential for nepotism can develop, they may need to consider other employment or take a transfer in job assignment so the conflict of interest is eliminated.

SCENARIO 6
She Is Making Me Feel Strange!

Type of Library: Any

Area of Library: Public Services: circulation/ILL

It was about 10:00 a.m. on a Friday morning when circulation supervisor Susan James heard a knock at her office door.

"Can I please talk to you?" came a hesitant voice. Susan immediately recognized it as belonging to Amy Lin, her longtime reserves assistant.

"Sure, come on in," Susan replied. "Is anything the matter?"

"Yes, but I don't really know how to say this," Amy began. "She's making me feel strange, I mean uncomfortable, I mean . . . but she's really a nice person."

"So Amy, what is going on?" said Susan in a comforting tone, with the intent of allowing Amy, who was visibly upset, to open up.

"It's Jessie Green, the new girl in ILL. She's being too, like, friendly; I mean it's not that I don't want people to be friendly, just not like that."

"Like what, Amy?" Susan insisted. "You're going to have to be more specific if you want me to help you."

Amy replied, measuring every word carefully. "The other day I was at my desk, and Jessie came over to talk with me about an ILL request I'd submitted for a community borrower, and as she bent over me, she put her arm around me. Then, as she got ready to leave, she tickled the back of my neck with her fingers."

"Did you say anything to her?" asked Susan.

"No," Amy replied. "I was so shocked that I just sat there stunned. Then she came in yesterday and began to stroke my back and hair, telling me how special I was and how she'd really like to get to know me better. I told her I thought she was OK, but I didn't like being touched that way."

"What did she say then?" Susan asked.

"She told me she was just being friendly and I shouldn't be so uptight, that we could be really good for each other, that she could help me overcome my fears. Susan, I'm not sure, but I think she may want to be more than friends! What if someone saw her rubbing my back? What would people think? What am I going to do?" By this time Amy was crying and hugging herself.

"First of all," Susan responded, "how did you react to her comment?"

"I told Jessie that I was not interested in anything like that, but she laughed and told me to calm down; we could talk about it later. She also said she didn't give up easy. She seems to think I'm scared but willing, and that's not it at all! I don't know how to handle this!"

Susan sat back in her chair and thought, "I need to handle this carefully, but how? How do I approach this with the least upset possible? It wouldn't do for this to become common knowledge, and I've got to be fair to Jessie as well."

Pat's Assessment

These days, sexual harassment is a topic that should be nothing new from the HR point of view. Every library should have a policy in place—usually derived from or mirroring that of the supporting institution. State law usually mandates these. This is where Susan should look for guidance. It is also a good idea to have a standard interview form to document the incident. This form will help ensure that all parties take the complaint seriously.

Workshops are often a good place to find out how to interpret guidelines, since some situations are difficult to assess. Libraries are a perfect breeding ground for harassment scenarios, some not so typical; harassment can take a number of twists and turns. Not all situations have clear-cut solutions.

For example, if the aggressor is not in a position to affect the victim's job, is it harassment? Some trainers say yes, some say no, and some say this falls under the heading of creating a hostile work environment. In other words, even if the aggressor is not responsible for the victim losing his or her job, any behavior that makes a reasonable person uncomfortable may still be considered harassment.

Another issue is how to resolve the problem of a "he said–she said" situation—how do you tell if people are telling the truth? Experts have different answers, but a favorite approach is to bring in credible investigators as soon as possible. This demonstrates to both parties that you are serious, offering support to the person telling the truth and putting the liar on notice. Such investigators know what they're doing and see these situations all the time. It is the organization's response to the situation that counts, and being fast and objective is of utmost importance. The trouble comes when institutions try to hide persistent problems.

A third issue is the touchy debate about the victim's responsibility. Feminists, sociologists, and political types say, "Don't blame the victim." The behaviorists and cognitive scientists say, "Learn to take responsibility." However, everyone agrees that if the aggressor does not take no for an answer, it is not the victim's fault.

Trainers also make sure that the staff know that assaults such as rape are about power, not sex. Although male-female scenarios are common, female-male, male-male, or female-female assaults also occur.

If this library has a carefully constructed policy for dealing with sexual harassment cases, Susan will be well prepared when Amy first comes in to talk. She should remain calm, pull a copy of the interview form from her files, and ask Amy to go through the questionnaire with her. She needs to inform Amy that the next step would be to interview Jessie. Although at this point Susan is not sure a law is being broken, she has to act as if it were. One trainer suggests that managers behave as if they might someday have to sit in a televised courtroom, justifying their actions.

Susan should use the interview form when she speaks with Jessie. Because of the potential legal issues, if Jessie denies everything, Susan will have to take official action. Susan should tell her this—often the possibility of legal action inspires honesty. Jessie may confess that perhaps she had been flirting a little strongly with Amy.

After individual interviews, Susan should call a meeting with Jessie, Amy, and a representative from human resources, and Susan should attend. The meeting should be documented and should give Jessie and Amy the chance to agree to try to work together without further misunderstanding.

Glenda's Assessment

PERSPECTIVES

Amy: I don't blame Susan for this; so there's nothing she could have done differently, but I wish Susan could do something to stop Jessie. I don't want her to tell Jessie that I told her.

Susan: First of all, it is simply Amy's word against that of Jessie, and I cannot assume that she is interpreting Jessie's behavior accurately. It is possible that Jessie intended no sexual meanings or that Amy overdramatized her behavior in describing it to me. Further, I cannot investigate it without revealing my source, since there were no witnesses. Since Jessie has no authority over Amy, it is not clear that Amy's refusal would have any impact on Amy's career. So there is a question as to whether sexual harassment has actually occurred. I will explain these considerations to Amy and give her a copy of our sexual harassment policy brochure, inviting her to share it with Jessie should there be any recurrence. I would then refer Amy to the employee assistance program for help in dealing with her feelings and in working out assertive strategies. I would suggest that Amy warn Jessie that if she persists, her behavior will be reported through official channels.

SUGGESTIONS FROM AN EMPLOYEE
ASSISTANCE PERSPECTIVE

Since we do not know whether an actual sexual gesture occurred, and since confidentiality is an issue, it is difficult to specify exactly what should be done at this point. It seems that the main need is for education at all levels—for all characters. If clear guidelines about sexual harassment are taught to the entire staff, clarity should result. If formal guidelines exist, Susan should follow them. If not, she might suggest that specific guidelines be developed.

In regard to the current situation, Susan should explain to Amy that she can do nothing about the situation unless she has permission to discuss it with Jessie. She can explain to Amy that she needs to be assertive and that if she is experiencing fear and other discomfort, she can go to the employee assistance counselor to work with these feelings and to get help in improving her assertiveness skills.

[*Legal disclaimer:* Supervisors should follow any existing procedures already in place at their institution.]

Authors' View

Sexual harassment is one area where most institutions now have at least some guidelines in place. Whether or not they are taken seriously by the institution can be another matter. If for some reason you cannot find adequate guidelines to assist you, find out what your state law says on the subject. For too long, sexual harassment was not addressed adequately in the workplace. Then, for a time, the pendulum swung the other way, and there were "witch hunts" against perceived offenders. Things have settled down and leveled out in most areas, although not necessarily where you work.

Be careful not to blow a situation out of its original proportion, but on the other hand, don't avoid it either because it appears awkward. It's possible for romantic "crushes" to turn ugly, but many times they simply run their course. Recipients of unwanted attention need to find ways to firmly make their disinterest known without falling victim to a cycle of harassment. A supervisor can assist the victim with the proper way to respond once the supervisor is versed in the subject and in the specifics of the individual case. Certainly not all such encounters require legal action, but inaction on the part of a supervisor can invite professional disaster. Above all, let the employee know that you are available to help if he or she requests your assistance. The employee may need guidance to wade through this emotional quagmire. In some cases, however, professional legal or psychological help, or both, is warranted. As supervisor, you can intervene in some ways, but do not get in over your head or allow yourself to be drawn into an interpersonal conflict you may not really understand. Any situation where there is a threat involved requires immediate, professional intervention. And in all cases, follow proscribed guidelines if there is any question.

SCENARIO 7
Useless, Totally Useless!

Type of Library: University library

Area of Library: Administration, cross-departmental

"How did it go?" Ted Cline asked sheepishly as his colleague and fellow department head, Molly Shapiro, entered the office suite they shared.

"He's useless, totally useless!" Molly exclaimed. "When he's not micromanaging some insignificant project, he's refusing to take a position on something that matters! I don't know why any of us bother to take a problem to him! You can't get a straight answer, let alone a decision!"

Ted had heard this anger and frustration before. He'd seen it on the faces of the other librarians and felt it himself on several occasions. Molly was, of course, referring to Bill Singer, the director of libraries at Whatsamatta University. Bill was known publicly as a genial man, socially astute and popular with the faculty. However, to his librarians and support staff, he was a source of ongoing frustration. Bill had trouble dealing with issues and making decisions involving personnel, conflicts, or even performance. "I don't like dealing with this stuff!" librarians had heard him declare when pushed for a decision. "I'm sure if we just give it a little time, it will sort itself out" was his favorite solution. This hopeful prediction rarely came true, and the library, as a consequence, was a cauldron of stress, frustration, and conflict.

"Well, he's going to have to listen to this one," Ted remarked. "We can't keep moving Bobbie around, hoping she'll finally find a place where she fits. I have a meeting with him at 3:00 p.m. today." Ted was referring to Bobbie Mattson, a longtime employee who never seemed to be able to make a success of her job assignment. In ill health and known for her sour disposition, for the last fifteen years Bobbie had been moved from department to department, position to position, in the hopes of finding a place where her "talents" could be employed. She would begin on a positive note, but soon she would be underperforming or would stir up some sort of trouble with the other employees. Bobbie seemed oblivious to her role in any conflict and saw herself as a perpetual victim. Each time a supervisor would collect enough evidence to start disciplinary proceedings, Bill would refuse to take action.

This time, however, Ted felt he had a solid case for action. He had, by accident, discovered dozens of undeposited library donor gift checks stashed in the back of a file drawer in Bobbie's work area. Surely, Ted reasoned, Bill could not ignore such a blatant financial transgression. This was costing the library thousands of dollars and mountains of goodwill with the community as donors' checks went unacknowledged and undeposited. When he confronted Bobbie about what he had found that past Friday, she burst into tears and fled to the bathroom. She had been out on sick leave ever since. Today was Wednesday. Ted knew he couldn't let this situation go unresolved and neither, he reasoned, could Bill.

"Well, good luck!" Molly said sarcastically as Ted left for the director's office. "I hope you get the support you need!" Ted waved and hurried down the hall.

"Come in, Ted, and sit down. What did you need to see me about on such short notice?" Bill said pleasantly.

"I wish I had good news, but I don't," said Ted. As he began to present the circumstances of Bobbie's latest mess, Bill remained silent except for an occasional deep sigh.

"Ted," he finally said, "what do you want me to do? Bobbie may not be the best employee we've ever had, but if we fire her, where would she go? It's not like there are jobs growing on trees for people like Bobbie. Do you really want to see her put out on the street? Do we really want to go through the whole painful process of termination? How will that look to the community? I hate dealing with this sort of thing!"

Ted felt his stomach churn and the hair on his neck bristle. "Bobbie's economic welfare is not our concern!" he blurted out. "She's had fifteen years and countless chances to improve her performance. Our concerns should be the efficient operation of this library and the morale of the other staff. How does it look to them if she's allowed to get away with this? Why should they care about their own performance when Bobbie is never held accountable? We cannot allow this incident to pass!"

"Don't you tell me how I should run this institution!" Bill snapped angrily, leaning forward to make his point. "May I remind you that you work for me and are not yet tenured! This conversation is over!" Bill glared at Ted, who by this time was slumped in the chair, staring at the floor. Bill opened and held the door for Ted as he shuffled out and back down the hall.

As he entered the office, Molly said softly, "How did it go?"
"I give up!" sighed Ted as he dropped into his chair. "I just give up!"

Pat's Assessment

It is clear to Ted that Bobbie's poor performance is a symptom of Bill's behavior as a director and of the behavior of everyone in the library. It is much
easier for everyone to be cynical and blame Bill for all these problems rather
than see how they are all part of a larger problem.

Ted also knows that if he wants to change the culture of the library, he
needs allies inside and outside the library. Ted wants to have solid political
advice and people who can back him up if a major blowup occurs. Also, he
needs champions who are leaders high up enough in the university chain of
command to influence Bill's behavior. Ted should find allies in department
chairs and deans, if possible, who share his concerns. Also, if he finds more
than one significant power in the community concerned with Bill's track
record, all the better.

A good way for Ted to start would be to carefully pick three colleagues
who are interested in action, not endless gossip. They all can band together
to remedy the situation if they are willing to take some risks together and
bear the consequences of their actions.

Next, Ted should consider his own job satisfaction. If he is considering
quitting, he should use the following list to help him decide whether it is
time to leave.

There are eight reasons to quit a job:

1. You become bitter.
2. You stop learning.
3. You are no longer making a contribution.
4. You are using drugs or alcohol or you are expected to work for
   someone who is an addict.
5. You find yourself lying, cheating, or stealing or violating your
   employer's value system, or you are asked to do so.
6. Your health is being affected by the stress of the job.
7. You intervene with difficult people and carry the burden of the
   emotional health of the organization.
8. You do not respect your supervisor, manager, director, or colleagues.

Ted should consider how his decision will affect his family and discuss frankly with them the long-term and short-term sacrifices if he quits his job or is fired, keeping in mind that the tenure process has checks and balances in place, and although Bill could make things difficult for him, he does not have total control over the outcome when it is time for Ted to be reviewed by the library's promotion and tenure committee. Over several weeks, the family should put together a strategic plan that includes investigating a shift of Ted's health insurance from the university to his wife's employer, scaling back on vacation expenditures, and reassessing their children's college plans. Ted should set a specific deadline for improvement before he finalizes his decision to leave. This will give him time to make plans. In the meantime, he can get his résumé in shape and discreetly begin job hunting on the side.

Once Ted's private life is in order, there are several ways he can help Bill make decisions. One is being willing to take the full responsibility for a decision.

By the end of the year, with Ted's self-imposed deadline approaching, he will find himself in a good position. Work is better, because he and others are not obsessing about Bill's flaws. Most of the department heads are willing to calmly take some risks by making decisions and reporting them to Bill in a matter-of-fact way, ignoring Bill's temper tantrums. Ted's job search should have turned up several interesting possibilities, and this can boost his self-esteem and get him ready to take another stab at the Bobbie problem.

Before going to Bill, he should fill in his champions and mentors to get their support. He should deliver documentation of Bobbie's transgressions, plus a copy of the university's regulations dealing with such matters; leave it for Bill to read in private; and then return to see him the next morning. Bill will likely waffle, as he has in previous confrontations, so Ted should be ready to lay his bombshell: Ted says he understands Bill's concerns, but he is sure that Bill knows that the library is obligated to report the incident, which is a potential felony because of the amount of money withheld. Ted says that he is happy to act as Bill's agent in the matter. Ted should keep copies of the report and inform Bill that the other copies will be sent out, as per the law, to the institution's lawyer, personnel department, and the dean.

If Ted is careful not to lose his temper, and makes sure that the reports are written to make Bill look good, he will be able to come out on top of this situation. Even if Bill manages to have him fired, Ted can rest easy knowing he's done the right thing and that Bobbie will not survive this incident as an employee.

Glenda's Assessment

PERSPECTIVES

Ted: Bill is known within the library as useless despite his popularity outside the library. He has been absolutely no help to me or to the other department heads. What could he have done to avoid bringing me to this point? He could have done the job he is paid to do! I have adequate proof of Bobbie's lack of performance and of the regulations she has violated. If Bill does not take action this time, I intend to report the entire matter to the Human Resources Department and also to the provost and then resign from my job. I can't stand this frustration any longer!

Bill: I don't see what all the fuss is about! It's no big deal that Bobbie has procrastinated in depositing the checks; it is obvious that she is not taking the money for her own use. I don't dare put the poor woman out on the street. Besides, why was Ted looking in her desk drawer anyway? I could get him for invading her space! Ted has threatened before and always backed down, so I have no reason to believe he will do anything this time. I'll just let it go and assume nothing is going to happen.

SUGGESTIONS FROM AN EMPLOYEE ASSISTANCE PERSPECTIVE

A manager should be open to reason, and *Conflict Management for Libraries* is designed to help reasonable managers learn to be open to reason. I don't think Bill is going to read any books on conflict management; therefore, I assume he isn't going to do anything and will either get by with it, as happens at some universities, or get fired! Thus, this question regards Ted's personal response to his manager rather than to a management question of his own.

I agree that Ted might have to resign and search for another job. I think it highly unlikely that Bill will make any changes. Perhaps the best course of action would be for Ted to seek counseling in the employee assistance program to help him work on his decision and his efforts to seek further employment. He will probably need some assistance for his family as well, since they may be uprooted and may have some major adjustments to make.

Authors' View

There are times when you must draw the line. If you work for someone who is too weak to make decisions that need to be made, find ways to make them yourself, or get out of the situation. As suggested above, there can be strength in numbers. But if the weakness is perpetuated up the line, then it becomes even more difficult to support bad management. This is especially true if the administration is looking the other way about serious policy and procedures infractions or in the worst-case scenario, criminal behavior. To-day's corporate climate suggests that taking the high road is always the better choice in the long run, even if the results are painful for the imme-diate future. It's better to lose a job than to be implicated in a scandal and possibly land in jail. An individual must, in the end, look after his or her own future. Your professional reputation will follow you for the duration of your working life. In a situation like the one described above, the individual may wish to quietly move on and let the chips fall where they may, minimizing the emotional toll on their physical and emotional health.

This advice should not be taken lightly. Finding another job in a slug-gish economy can be a risky business—however, not being able to live with your conscience is also likely to take its toll on your health and your life if you try to bury such situations inside yourself. Sometimes a discreet, yet de-liberate job search will provide you the life options needed for a respon-sible, well-reasoned, and productive decision regarding your current situa-tion. It's up to you!

SCENARIO 8
Let Me Do My Job!

Type of Library: Suburban public library

Area of Library: Administration and board

Amanda Jones paced her office, furious at what had transpired. The Library Advisory Board of the Bennigan County Public Library System was at it again. She thought angrily, "Does anyone want to look up the word *advisory* in the dictionary?" Amanda's philosophy and all of her experience sug-gested that the board's role was to assist and advise but not to dictate. Amanda had plenty of experience running a library—this was her third direc-torship—but she had never encountered a board so bent on telling her how to do her job.

She was disgusted when Olive Mason, chair of the board, had interfered with a recent hire. Last month when a new reference support staff position was open, Olive had come to see Amanda. She made no bones about the reason for her visit.

"Amanda, dear, my friend Sylvia Murphy's daughter Alice will be applying for your open staff position. She's such a lovely girl, and she just graduated from that nice little college in Livingston. I'm sure you'll find her to be a perfect fit. I told her how much I thought of you and that the library would be such an interesting place to work."

"So, does Alice have any library experience? Perhaps at the college?" Amanda asked.

"Oh, I don't think so. But she loves to read, and she is such a sweet girl," Olive replied.

Amanda frowned. "Well, Olive, we'll probably have quite a few candidates. You know, this is not an entry-level position. We need someone with at least some library experience. Since we're so close to Watertown, and there are several library science programs within a one-hundred-mile radius, we are blessed with strong pools of candidates when we advertise. Do you think your friend's daughter might want to go into librarianship someday?"

Olive's reaction gave Amanda the chills. "Dear," she said in a quiet, serious tone, "I don't think you understand me. Alice is your girl. I've already spoken with Doris Finley down at Human Resources, and she said she would flag Alice's application. Besides, it's just a support staff position, isn't it? She'll be fine."

Amanda knew that Olive wasn't kidding and that she really was expecting Amanda to hire this totally inexperienced applicant, sight unseen, because of her connections to Olive.

"Olive, I can't promise anything. We strive to adhere to fair hiring practices, and although I will consider interviewing this young lady, it will depend on how she compares to other qualified applicants."

As it turned out, there were several excellent applicants for the position, but somehow it was Alice who was hired. Apparently, Olive further lobbied the staff behind Amanda's back. It also came to light that the head of reference's daughter and Alice were good friends. Although Alice did turn out to be competent, Amanda was not comfortable with the turn of events. This was not the way she conducted job searches, and she did not want it to happen this way again. It gave her the feeling that somehow she was losing control of her own library.

Today's advisory board meeting made her realize that she wasn't being paranoid. Jim Watts, the local owner of the Building Supply Depot, was another member of the board who apparently decided that he knew how to run a library.

"Amanda, we are so excited about getting Morgan Murdock's collection of furniture and landscaping books for the library's collection."

"What collection are you talking about, Jim?" Amanda wanted to know.

"Oh, Morgan is an old friend of mine. You know, he's been coming in to our store ever since we were just a little town hardware store. He's amassed quite a collection of books on all kinds of home improvement projects and renovation—you know, all that kind of great stuff. He's retiring and is getting ready to sell his house and move to Florida. I told him the library would be thrilled to take his collection. He won't need them down in that retirement community. There are about twenty-five boxes of books. Oh yes, I just remembered—he also wants an inventory list and an appraisal before he leaves next week. I'm sure your staff can handle that, right?"

Amanda flushed. "Jim, how long have you been on the library advisory board? Four years? Have you ever thought to ask about the library's gift policy before you go promising things?"

"But Amanda," Jim looked honestly perplexed. "I thought you would love to have this collection. I wouldn't have considered accepting it if I didn't think it would be great for the library."

"And maybe it will be great," Amanda replied. "But as a board member, your responsibility is to come back to us with information, and we make the decision together, and with gifts such as this, we must include the staff and the collection development librarian. Norma and her staff really will not be happy knowing that you are trying to do their job. And he needs an appraisal and a list next week? Isn't this a little short notice? Furthermore, we cannot legally handle appraisals—that is the donor's responsibility—and if you had thought about it at all you would have realized that."

Jim looked downcast for a minute and then brightened. "Well, I can help Morgan find an appraiser. I have a buddy who owns a used bookstore who does them all the time. But I did tell him we'd be taking the books, and I told him someone from the library would be able to pick them up by the end of the week."

Amanda sighed. How was she ever going to get this group under control? She knew these two incidents were the tip of the iceberg. It was only a matter of time before the others on the board would be taking library matters into their own hands.

Pat's Assessment

Amanda's situation with her board evolved because of her and the board's collective lack of interest in board training. She needs to contact her local library system, her state library association, her state library, and ALA's Association for Library Trustees and Advocates (ALTA) for assistance. A grant from her state library can give her the money to hire a trainer, who can come out to her library and conduct an all-day, on-site retreat for the board and the staff of the library. The personnel officer of the county can come too, as should one of the elected county commissioners. A staff member from the state library can also be there to explain the more obscure parts of their state's library law.

Amanda and her board members need a surprisingly disciplined education in the behavior of advisory boards in their state. The most important lesson is appreciating and differentiating among the roles of the advisory board, the director, and the staff. The advisory board members need to learn that even if they are an administrative board, it does not mean they are allowed to run the library. Their job? A few highlights:

Create, with the input of the staff and community, and with the partnership of the director, a strategic plan to help chart the future of the library

Use the strategic plan as a foundation, to create benchmarks for evaluating the director and reporting the yearly results to the county commissioners

Help promote the library to the greater community

Be an advocate of the library to the county commissioners

Notice the board does *not* get to run the library or hire, evaluate, or fire staff. The director has to run the library. But, given that, the director needs to partner in leadership with the board. Amanda needs a reminder that even if she is the best director on the planet, she is still a government employee who needs to have a way of responding to the needs of the taxpayers who pay her salary and the community she serves, including children, business owners, the homeless, tourists, and visitors to the town. Governance is a balancing act, and her professional training and experience are only part of the picture.

And what is the job of the staff? The staff members of the library are the eyes, ears, and hands. They provide immediate input to the director about what is happening in the library—another part of the balancing act.

And, although the board is not allowed to interfere with running the library, a well-thought-out grievance policy means that the staff can have access to the board in case of problems with the director.

Even if the board training is a success, it is likely that at least one board member will discount the information from the trainer and the state representative. Amanda can recruit the remaining board members to stand up to the difficult board member and keep him or her on track. Amanda will also need to spend more time politicking with the county commissioners, who are her real bosses. The county's top manager and the Human Resources Department people will be sympathetic once they realize what is happening. As long as those difficult board members are on the board, Amanda has to be extra careful to communicate decisions to both the county administrative team and the advisory board members at the same time, to delegate a little more, and to be more open to listening to her board's concerns.

Glenda's Assessment

PERSPECTIVE

Amanda: I wish I had conducted a board training program. I realize now that I probably let them get by without board training when I really should have insisted on the appropriate programs. But blaming myself now is no good, and whining and calling myself a victim won't help either. So what shall I do?

Since Alice has already been hired, there's nothing I can do about that. But I can tell Jim that I will not send a library staff member to pick up the books. He can go ahead with the appraisal and follow standard procedures to assess whether the collection will be accepted. In the meantime, I'll collect state laws regarding hiring decisions, library procedures, and such and distribute them to the board. I'll then schedule a board-training workshop to cover procedures and to make certain that no one takes control of my job. If in the future there are staff openings, I will follow correct procedures in setting up a screening committee and in conducting interviews, allowing people to be interviewed only if their credentials passed a checklist of requirements listed in the job advertisement. Further, I will set up a checklist of procedures to use in making a decision regarding accepting or declining gift collections offered to the library. I will make it clear to the board that we are legally required to meet standards and to keep the public informed about these procedures. If the board does not agree to follow carefully written policies and procedures, I shall resign!

SUGGESTIONS FROM AN EMPLOYEE
ASSISTANCE PERSPECTIVE

Little in this scenario lends itself to an employee assistance program except for the likely possibility that Amanda will need supportive counseling and also help with decision making should she start looking for a job change.

Authors' View

There's an old saying that it is easier to get forgiveness than to ask permission. Amanda's board members will continue to go beyond their bounds if they don't have guidelines to follow or if they feel they can easily ignore the existing ones without consequence. Amanda cannot blame them if she does not stay on top of what is going on and establish guidelines soon. This scenario is also about personal and professional boundaries, and as with the art of raising children, effective and fair boundaries must be established for adult behaviors and personal interactions. On the other hand, Amanda also needs to personally examine her own specific management style and her desire for control and willingly consider the opportunities her board members present from time to time. Making sure that everyone is on the same page with hiring practices, donation policies and procedures, and other rules and regulations will go a long way in preserving good relations and avoiding misunderstandings.

SCENARIO 9
What Is Taking Those People So Long?

Type of Library: Public library

Area of Library: Technical Services and Public Services conflict

"I don't get it! What is so darned complicated about cataloging a book?" exclaimed Walter Grimance, head of reference at LaRue Valley Public Library, to his colleague, Caitlin Fostex, head of Access Services, as they walked into the neighborhood coffee shop. "I sometimes believe they are pulling the biggest con job in this library district! The problem is that none of us know enough to call their bluff. They don't seem to work down there." He added, "Every time I go down to check on a title, they're sitting around talking and taking their own sweet time while the rest of us have to answer to angry patrons! I tell you, they have carved out a plum job for themselves and made their area into a sacred cow that can't be touched!"

"Come on, Walter; it's not that bad," Caitlin laughed, trying to lighten the mood. "I hated cataloging in library school. I'm happy somebody wants to do it. What happened this time?"

Walter sank into his chair, sipping his coffee. "Six weeks ago I ordered a book for Harry Baggawynd, our favorite local history buff. It arrived in two weeks because Joey in acquisitions sent the order as a 'rush.' But for a solid month the book has sat in cataloging while Mina Bellinger and her group work their magic with it, and it's still not ready. Jeepers! You'd think it was a rare tome found in a pyramid of Egypt. I've complained to the director, but she refuses to force the issue, and Mina accuses me of asking her to lower her standards. What standards? I know they get most of the records from OCLC, so what is taking so long? I've got twice the education as the best cataloger down there, and I'll bet I could have had the book signed, sealed, and delivered by now."

"Walter, you are a hoot!" chuckled Caitlin. But she knew Walter's frustration. Books did seem to linger in cataloging for long periods after they were received. Patrons and public service librarians had complained to Mina, head of the cataloging unit, and to Delia Demerest, the director of libraries, but every time, Mina would lapse into a diatribe about cataloging standards. Everyone's eyes glazed over during her monologues about OCLC searching costs, consortia agreements, access points, and authority control issues, ad nauseam. Delia would invariably back Mina and her standards.

"Delia doesn't want to make a fuss, and she hasn't a clue what Mina is talking about," Caitlin sighed. "Walter, I'm afraid this one has beaten you, so don't get worked up over it! Maybe, after Delia retires, the new director will outsource cataloging! It can't be any worse than what we have now."

"I live for that day!" Walter exclaimed as they finished their coffee and headed back to the library.

Pat's Assessment

To attack this problem head-on, the weary director, Delia Demerest, will have to untangle the reasons for the different departments getting on each other's nerves. There seemed something primal about it, something more than the librarians trying to establish who is the most important animal on the totem pole. She can begin by sketching out the most common complaints her staff bring her about each other:

Circulation: "We are the ones who have to deal with all of the crazies and have the most pressure to perform. Yet the line can be back up to the door and those lazy prima donnas in reference won't move off their butts."

Reference: "We are the heart of the library, but no one appreciates us anymore. Where we go, the library goes. And those people in Children's Services want to turn this place into a day-care center! Is there any way we can legally keep them out?"

Children's Services: "Children's Services is the heart and soul of the library. We need more space, more books, and more staff! We need people to monitor the parents! Not everyone can deal with children, you know. It takes a special talent that the average parent does not have. We are the stepchild of library service—no one respects us."

Cataloging: "Studies have shown that the philosophical and intellectual heart of the library is cataloging. Without order, there is no reason. We suspect God was a cataloger—just reread the first chapters of Genesis. We will not lower our standards to compromise the austere beauty of our order! If the patrons can't understand our logic, educate them or ignore them."

Systems Support: "Why are we the only people in this library who know how to turn on a computer or check that it is plugged in? Are we the only ones living in the twenty-first century as opposed to the eighteenth century? Those fools in other departments should not be allowed to have drivers' licenses. Look what they are doing to our beautiful machines! Why don't they check the help menu before they call? Why don't they come to classes? Why don't they care?"

Administration: "If everyone would just follow the rules, there would be no wars. Oh, and if everyone would just fill out their time cards and insurance forms correctly, there would be peace in the world."

Acquisitions: "No one cares about us. Most of us don't have MLS degrees, and we are better people for not having gone to college. All card-carrying librarians are snobs, particularly the ones who work in Technical Services. We may be accountants and clerks, and we may deal with the routine work, but we are convinced that library school removes people's common sense. Why can't a reference librarian with an MLS figure out how to fill out an order form correctly? Why can't they read the labels on the shelves and actually put a book that needs to be dealt with in the back room in the right section? Oh, and have any of them ever really done anything for a living, besides talk? We'd like to see them check in a new shipment of books in the time they expect us to do it!"

Clearly, the main problem is that all staff members think their jobs are about their department, their functions, their "professionalism," and their turf. The sense of responsibility Delia wants her employees to have has deteriorated into territory building. She needs to get everyone to understand that building the perfect library is not the goal; serving the needs of the patrons is the goal. This will mean collaboration and communication between the departments.

Delia and her staff need to attack the problem on two levels. At one level, they need to create strategic plans that reflect goals of the library and the customers it serves, not the issue of whose job is more important or whose degree or training is more prestigious. The second level is that everyone needs to better understand the jobs of the other employees. For example, why did the Reference Department organize the reference books in several sections that were not 100 percent in Dewey decimal classification order? Or what did the children singing during story hour have to do with literacy? Delia's first step will be to schedule a regular, one-hour, monthly all-staff meeting, during each of which an individual from a different department stands up and explains his or her work and day-to-day activities.

Second, Delia can schedule a retreat for top managers and bring in an outside facilitator. The retreat should allow the participants to get better ideas of everyone else's priorities, give the participants the opportunity to comment on what other people are doing, and identify areas where compromise and collaboration are the keys, based on the strategic plan.

Some sound bites from the workshop:

> *Reference:* "We can cross-train other staff and librarians to help out with our work, even if they are not experienced reference librarians, and we can make sure we communicate better with other departments."
>
> *Children's Services:* "We can find ways to ensure that the kids do not terrorize the rest of the library and can work on librarywide

signage to communicate what is happening in Children's Services."

Cataloging: "We can create tiers of work, based on the needs of the rest of the library. So, for most of the items, we will use all of the OCLC shortcuts, and we will get them out ASAP. We promise to meet the agreed turnaround deadlines or investigate outsourcing."

Systems Support: "We will create more instructional sheets and ten-minute trainings. Also, we will be more realistic with our budget and personnel and improve our teaching and training methods."

Glenda's Assessment

PERSPECTIVES

Walter: I can't understand why Harry Baggawynd is blaming me for the delay in receiving the book he ordered. It's hard to explain to a regular patron that I did my job in a timely fashion but that those lazy bums in cataloging are making me look bad! It does no good to complain to Delia because she just lets those folks sit and twiddle their thumbs instead of working! She's really not doing her job either! I wish Delia would call those folks in cataloging on the carpet and explain that they are making the rest of us look like fools. Wouldn't you think Delia wouldn't want the whole library to look bad to the community? She just needs to force them to do their jobs.

Delia: Unfortunately, this isn't just a local problem. I hear this from colleagues in libraries all over the country. It is difficult for any of us to understand how much time someone else's work takes, and we usually think people are just making excuses when they suggest that we want them to lower their standards. I know that I can't solve this problem totally, but it might be helpful if I talked with Mina to learn how much of a backlog her department has, how long it takes from the date they receive a book to the date they send it to the shelves, and how she supervises and evaluates her staff. She might take offense, but I do need this type of information if I am to supervise her appropriately. I need to know whether she is understaffed for the volume of cataloging required and whether she has on her staff some deadwood that needs to be cleaned out.

Not just because of this, but for many reasons, I plan to schedule annual team-building retreats so that personnel in different departments can get to know people they rarely meet. Hopefully, this will motivate them to try to understand the pressures on people in other departments.

SUGGESTIONS FROM AN EMPLOYEE ASSISTANCE PERSPECTIVE

Since it is clear that this is not a local problem, nor is it a problem unique to librarians, it appears that the best alternative is to consider it a human relations issue. In every library, including this one, leaders need to schedule frequent team-building activities. Employee assistance program counselors could be helpful in planning and implementing retreats and other activities for this purpose.

Authors' View

As long as anyone has the impression that the Cataloging Department takes too long cataloging books, or that acquisitions takes too long ordering them, or that reference librarians spend too much time reading the newspaper, then there is a perception problem, if nothing else. Such impressions tend to linger and become permanent in the minds of patrons. The director, Delia, probably understands the big picture better than anyone, and it's her job to help everyone understand it too.

This is not to say that there might not be a problem with the Cataloging Department's turnaround time in this particular library—Walter's complaint may be legitimate, but his characterization of the issue leads the reader to realize that he probably does not have a clue about what actually happens in the cataloging process. Perhaps if he did, he could be more sympathetic—and could articulate the delay with the request better to Harry Baggawynd. There could be other factors at play in this issue. As many cataloging staffs have been downsized, catalogers are caught in the dilemma of maintaining standards while trying to do more with less. The same could be true for acquisitions as well. The catalogers, on the other hand, must understand that "rush" means getting the book in the hands of the requesting reader ASAP, and the finer points of the bibliographic record can be sweated over at a later time. Instead of grousing to his public services coworker, Walter should be talking to Mina to find out why this particular book cannot be expedited for this patron who is obviously a regular in the library. No book that is not problematic in some way takes a month to catalog; either

Walter is exaggerating or something is wrong—perhaps someone is out on extended leave and it's sitting on his or her desk, the book has been mis-filed in the backlog and has lost its "rush" flag, or something equally as in-nocent but obviously problematic has happened to prevent the cataloging from being completed. Direct communication can solve many problems be-fore they become overwhelming or embarrassing to all involved.

Walter should be able to feel comfortable approaching Mina with this sort of request. If Mina is not cooperative, something needs to change. All sections of the library need to work together and realize that they are each other's customers many times as much as they are all there to serve the users.

SCENARIO 10
I've Got a Great Idea for You!

Type of Library: University library

Area of Library: Cross-departmental, Technical Services and Reference

Head of Technical Services Joan Clausen had settled into dealing with annual report statistics (which were due the next day) when she heard a knock. "Come in," Joan called out, hoping whatever it was wouldn't take long.

"Joan, I've got a great idea for you," exclaimed Ron Stampel, head of Reference Services. Ron was a highly educated, likable fellow, a good li-brarian who seemed to have a great deal of time on his hands. Ron was helpful and generous with his advice even when it wasn't solicited.

"You know how the university accounting office took those funds away at the end of the last fiscal year because we didn't spend them? All you need to do here in Technical Services is to overspend the budget, say, by 50 percent or more, and you're sure not to lose any this year!" Ron announced as he leaned back in the office chair, obviously proud of himself.

"That's an interesting idea, Ron," Joan replied. "But there are some other factors to consider. First of all, we'd run the risk of seriously depleting next year's appropriation, encumbering much of it to pay for older orders, not to mention what will happen if our budget remains static. We also would run into the problems associated with accounts being put on hold by ven-dors as invoices pile up and go unpaid. Subscriptions would have to be can-celed, and then, once we get the new appropriation, we'd spend a lot of time and energy repairing the damage done by significantly overextending the budget. I would agree, however, that for accounts payable to take encumbered funds back demonstrates a lack of foresight. Maybe we can take that topic up with them in a meeting sometime.

"Also, Ron, as you know, it often takes up to ninety days for us to receive a new fiscal year's budget. Invoices can take another thirty days to make it through accounts payable. Vendors can and do resent outstanding balances of that duration."

"Hey, if they want their money, they'll just have to wait for it!" Ron laughed. "Anyway, I was just trying to help. Oh, by the way," Ron said as he got up to leave, "I've already spoken to the dean about my idea. She said she'll be calling you soon."

Ron closed the door and disappeared down the hall. Joan's teeth clenched. "Just what I needed," Joan thought. "Not only have I lost a half hour with Ron, but now I'll be called to the dean's office to explain the whole thing to her!"

The phone rang. "Joan, this is Dean Frankenbaum. Ron Stampel was here, and he's got a great idea for how to manage our budget. Can you come to my office around 11:00 a.m. today? Great, see you then."

Joan hung the phone up slowly as her anger rose like a bonfire. "Great, just great!" she thought. "There goes my morning! Why can't people do the job they were hired to do and stay out of other people's business? This is the third time this semester public services people toddled down to our department with their great ideas and wreaked havoc in their wake. They must think we're idiots who can't tie our own shoelaces! They would have a cow if I pranced up to the reference desk and advised them on how to conduct a reference interview. How is it they can interfere and we can't? I've got to calm down," Joan thought to herself. "I can't go into the dean's office like this!"

Pat's Assessment

First, Joan needs to calm down and think about the situation from a larger point of view. Ron really does mean well, but his ideas come with a cost. An old trick might be helpful here:

Draw a square on a piece of paper and draw two crossing lines inside the box, creating four small boxes. In each of the boxes, write one of four words:

like, *dislike*, *right*, and *wrong*. When a situation comes up with someone at work, write the person's name above the boxes and make check marks in each box regarding your opinion of this person and his or her idea. This little exercise helps you keep a sense of perspective. In almost every difficult situation, someone is liked more than some other person, and someone is more right or more wrong. If you do the math, you find that with

Like	Dislike
Right	Wrong

these two sets of choices, Like and Dislike, Right and Wrong, there are at least four possibilities about each person. The most important thing to remember is that the person you like might be wrong, and the person you dislike might be right. You might be a nice person, but you might be wrong, and the other person might be right.

Joan's anger at Ron is hurting her ability to be objective. The mission is to improve customer service, not to protect the sanctity of her department.

Management is mostly about people, not systems. In fact, 50 percent of a typical supervisor's work involves people. So, Joan needs to plan her days around interruptions from people, including and especially Ron.

Joan needs to make appointments with Ron and the other department heads to discuss how Technical Services can better serve the library by modifying budget planning. At the same time, she can go to the dean and ask to have a meeting about communication among department heads. This meeting can cover the concern that each person can do a better job of copying ideas to each other in stages—input, discussion, and action—rather than making a decision and then telling the person after the fact that action was going to be taken.

Though Ron is not guaranteed to be a 100 percent happy camper during this process, he is likely to muffle his complaints if Joan remains pleasant and open to change. Because other department heads also have concerns about interruptions and being blindsided, the group should reach a consensus on making some simple changes.

Joan and Ron are fortunate to work for a library that has a working strategic plan (not just a dusty doorstop) and simple and reasonable systems in place to communicate and evaluate new ideas. An electronic list just for the purpose of discussing new ideas would be especially helpful. By creating an asynchronous discussion through an e-mail list, busy people like Joan can review ideas at their own convenience without being interrupted on hectic days.

Glenda's Assessment

PERSPECTIVES

Joan: I don't know what I could have done to prevent this feeling, but I am really upset! I have built up lots of resentment against Ron, and I'm having trouble sleeping nights. When he went to the dean, it was the last straw! I wish I had figured out a way to shut him up before it reached this point.

First, I'll find the written policies concerning the handling of budgets and ordering materials. I'll bet there are some written rules that prohibit what he is suggesting. I must be prepared to show this to the dean.

Second, I'll go to Ron and tell him that he can share all the ideas with me that he wants, and I'll listen and consider each one. But I insist that he avoid going over my head to provide suggestions for my department. I will also ask that he schedule appointments when he wants to share suggestions with me because he interrupted some urgent work. Then I'll talk myself into being firm with him if he interrupts me again.

Third, I'll join an exercise program and a support group and possibly go to the employee assistance program to get some help with cognitive processes and assertiveness skills. I should never have let him interrupt such an important task! I need to learn to say no and stick to it. I know that I'm making entirely too much of this and that Ron can't take advantage of me without my permission!

The Dean: I acknowledge that I should have told Ron to discuss this with Joan instead of my listening to his story. It really wasn't appropriate for me to listen to him and then summon Joan in the way that I did. I will apologize to Joan and avoid letting Ron sway me again. I trust Joan to make good decisions and recommendations, and I must make certain that she knows I trust her.

SUGGESTIONS FROM AN EMPLOYEE ASSISTANCE PERSPECTIVE

Joan should postpone the appointment with the dean so that she will have extra time to prepare herself for the session. She should see the employee assistance counselor and should focus on cognitive and relaxation strategies. After a few sessions, she will hopefully have developed a calm way to approach Ron about the need for him to share his ideas in appropriate ways.

When she has learned to calm herself and has studied budget procedures so that she is ready to see the dean, she should reschedule that appointment and be ready to evaluate Ron's suggestion from a fresh perspective.

Authors' View

There are two issues at play here: how to accept ideas from others, whether they are good ones or not, and how to work with someone who constantly goes over your head. The only way to stop interdepartmental one-upmanship and turf battles is to formalize certain communication values. We have seen this work wonders in many libraries. There must be an overall plan in place on which people can focus their attention. Whenever ideas for changes are put forth, this plan should be referenced. The downside of the process is that in order for everyone to be aware of what is going on, people must take the time to participate. This can draw out a process longer but does help everyone understand what is happening.

It can be very irritating to have a colleague who second-guesses you constantly. It is natural to feel threatened by others who seem to want to do your job for you. Having a colleague who goes over your head to your boss with ideas for improvement for something you are responsible for, well, that can ruin your day. It's important, therefore, to take a deep breath and try to focus on the big picture. The acquisitions budget, the information literacy program, or the rotation schedule for the computers—whatever it is—doesn't belong to you; it belongs to the library. Your colleague may make a ridiculous suggestion based on misinformation or total ignorance. It's your responsibility to help that person understand the big picture too. The more we know, the better we are able to make decisions together. Instead of hoarding information, share it. In the long run, the library benefits and people understand each other better.

SCENARIO 11
I'd Really Like to Help Donnie

Type of Library: Public library

Area of Library: All

"Oh dear," sighed Elaine Weeks, one of Bluestone Public Library's circulation assistants, as she laid the telephone receiver back in its cradle. "It's Donnie again—this time he wants us to look in the director's files for him after work."

"We can't do that!" exclaimed Jane Bell, her coworker. "What if some-one were to walk in and catch us? What if Mr. Worthy [Bob Worthy, the di-rector] were to return to the office?"

"I know, I know, but Donnie was always a good friend, and I feel really guilty not helping him on this one. Why did they have to fire him? He may not have been the most productive member of the staff, but he made up for it in good humor and support. I mean, he was there for me during my divorce."

Jane rested her head in her hands as she said, "I know what you mean. All of us knew Donnie didn't pull his weight, but you couldn't help liking the guy."

Elaine and Jane were in a real quandary that Friday afternoon. Donnie Schubert had been a likable member of the staff, popular with everyone but his supervisor. He did spend a lot of time wandering the halls and talking, so it didn't surprise people when they heard he'd been reprimanded. Every-one tried to take his probation seriously and even covered for Donnie when he wasn't at his desk and couldn't be located. Finally, the word came down that he had been asked to resign. Although Donnie took advantage of every internal grievance and appeal process available, the documentation pre-sented supporting the allegations that he spent more time on the job doing anything but his job held up throughout the process. Donnie was convinced that his supervisor fabricated some of the information, making him look far worse than the situation warranted. He was also sure that Director Worthy had something in writing that would prove his case, but all his requests for such proof thus far had turned up nothing.

Donnie began calling his friends at the library to let them know he was accusing the administration of "having it in for him." He told stories of verbal abuse from his supervisor, Sean Franklin, which shocked everyone and made them wary of Sean lest he turn on them the way he turned on "poor Donnie." One staff member was so enraged that she confronted Sean at a staff meeting, demanding to know why he had treated Donnie in such a manner. Even though Sean denied this allegation, the end result was that no one believed him, and the members of the staff no longer ate lunch with Sean or spoke to him unless absolutely necessary.

Donnie continued to call and talk to anyone who would listen about how he'd been abused and possibly discriminated against. Donnie's most recent theory—that he was being discriminated against because of his high IQ— had prompted him to ask Elaine to slip into the director's office during lunch, open the personnel files, and look for material that might help his case. Although Donnie already had an official copy of his own personnel file, he suspected that there were documents removed from it that would clear his case.

"I'm really scared," Elaine muttered to her office-mate Jane, "but I really want to help Donnie, in spite of the fact I know this request is out of bounds, and it could get me fired too!"

Pat's Assessment

It is clear that Donnie's behavior is causing a cascade of inappropriate behavior among staff members. However, Donnie cannot be made a scapegoat —everyone has to be held accountable for his or her workplace behavior.

Before the situation escalated, Bob could have used Donnie as a catalyst for a long-overdue overhaul of the library's personnel system. After all, everyone can benefit from paying better attention to productivity issues.

One common cause of productivity problems is that there are no criteria for productivity; thus, supervisors do not have the training necessary to effectively evaluate and coach employee behavior. If the library does not have a budget for organizational development, the administration can use the information already available to the library community and from workplace experts. Bob can enlist the Technical Services folks to delve into management magazines and books, circulation staff to check with local business contacts and professional associations, the Reference Department to do the online searches, and Automation Services staff to contact state libraries for comparison studies on productivity. Bob and the branch managers can go back to the library professional associations at the state and national levels and call on other library directors for advice. Each department should, in a year's time, put together a reasonable program of evaluation based on universally agreed-upon criteria with staff input and help from personnel experts and the city Human Services Department.

The library needs to implement a system that includes a series of awards and incentives to reinforce the hard work and thank people for a good job. That is the beauty of a good performance evaluation system—it increases the rewards for doing your job and behaving decently, lowers the amount of attention for bad behavior, and delineates the consequences for not doing your job and acting out. Also, it is based on some objective standards, so a person who is not liked but is doing his or her job will get a fairer hearing than the Donnies of the world, whom everyone likes but who are goldbricks.

When Donnie whispered allegations against his supervisor, his coworkers should have advised him to collect evidence and to document the information for the director. Since Donnie chose to ignore legitimate channels for grievances, he did not have documentation of his own and therefore no resources with which to fight back when presented with documented complaints about his work performance.

But Donnie is not the only problem here. What about Donnie's chorus of discontents who supported his dysfunctional behavior? We tend to overlook the circle of friends who fan the flames through gossip and unfounded accusations. The same system of training, performance evaluations, and clear communication on the part of the administration also can displace unhealthy behaviors. When people see solid evidence that behavior has consequences, both positive and negative; that complaints are taken seriously, that most of the time people are rewarded for their good behavior, that everyone has input in the decision-making processes of the library, and that the personnel rules are transparent, Donnie and those like him will have little influence.

Glenda's Assessment

PERSPECTIVES

Elaine: I am stuck between a rock and a hard place. I feel so helpless! One side of me knows that it would be wrong to sneak into the files, but the other side of me just can't say no to such a good friend. I am really angry with Sean for verbally abusing Donnie, and I'm mad at both Sean and Bob for firing him. I think Bob should have done something long ago instead of leaving it up to Sean. It is obvious that Sean wasn't clear about his expectations of Donnie. But I'm stuck with the decision about what to do about the files.

I wish Sean and Bob would call Donnie and invite him to come back for another chance, but I doubt this will happen. But they need to do something! Morale has hit rock bottom around here!

Sean: I feel simply awful! No one talks to me anymore, and I didn't do a thing to deserve this. I think Bob should have handled the thing with Donnie instead of dumping it on me. I did my best to help Donnie, but he just wouldn't listen. What gripes me the most now is that personnel issues are confidential, so I can't defend myself when people accuse me of being unfair to Donnie. Donnie can make up and spread any lies he wants, but I can't refute them.

I think Bob should call a meeting and tell everybody that what happened is not my fault! I have become a scapegoat.

Bob: I guess I screwed up. I thought Sean was up to the task of handling Donnie, and I underestimated the impact of Donnie's popularity with the other staff members. I wish I had anticipated the problem. I know I could have handled it better. But what can I do now?

First, I resolve to train my supervisors more effectively in the future. They need to learn to be very specific about expectations and evaluation of work and to keep on top of problems rather than letting them grow. Beginning now, I will meet periodically with each supervisor and find out where problems are cropping up. I'll help them to understand the importance of clear communication of expectations and specific evaluations that make each employee aware of possible performance problems and possible penalties for failure to meet expectations. I will insist that they document every step in writing with a signature showing that the employee has read each document.

But that doesn't solve our current morale problem. I will schedule a staffwide retreat with an outside facilitator to do some planning for how we want our workplace to function. When people raise questions about Donnie, I'll have to tell them that I cannot talk about confidential matters and just hope they'll accept that. If they blame Sean, I'll take responsibility instead of letting Sean take the blame, but I'm afraid that might fail. I will acknowledge that I did not plan adequately and that I am sorry. But we must move on. I'll know better next time!

SUGGESTIONS FROM AN EMPLOYEE ASSISTANCE PERSPECTIVE

Bob has the right idea. He should improve the training of supervisors and help them to design appropriate means of explaining expectations and evaluating work. He should meet periodically with each supervisor and should schedule a retreat with an outside facilitator. Unfortunately, he cannot talk about confidential personnel matters with his staff, resulting in the strong probability that they will perceive his behavior as unfair. Hopefully, the facilitator will provide opportunities for staff members to work toward greater harmony during the retreat, and Bob will have to accept the fact that it will take some time for him to show that he really is trustworthy. In the meantime, Elaine, Jane, and Sean might be encouraged to engage in individual counseling sessions to work through their feelings about this. Elaine, especially, may need help with the guilt she feels for not having been able to help Donnie.

Authors' View

This scenario, although certainly about Donnie, is also about his friends back at the library. Maybe Donnie's departure could have been avoided, or perhaps it could have happened even sooner. But the administrative choices made now affect everyone—so what about Elaine's predicament? She is confronted with a perceived injustice. Should she risk helping Donnie?

The portrait of Donnie painted in this scenario does not suggest that he was treated badly—certainly not as badly as he may have damaged the library and his friends. The fact that he has actually left of his own accord, though under duress, puts him at a disadvantage. The scenario does not make it clear whether Donnie deserves a second chance or not. But the question remaining has to do with Elaine and her coworkers. This seems to be a case of a well-meaning but destructive psychological entrapment developed in his coworker friends by Donnie and maintained by his enablers and now coconspirators in his attempt to secretly retrieve evidence that will supposedly clear his reputation. Should they try to help Donnie, and if so, how?

Elaine and her colleagues could have helped Donnie before things got out of hand by letting him know that his behavior was not appropriate in the workplace. However, they were lured by Donnie's uncanny ability to charm and distract them from their work with his jokes, stories, and general happy-go-lucky attitude. Donnie's infectious personality caused people to flock to him. Also, since it is exciting to be angry, fearful, and self-righteous, the drama of Donnie gave people a form of self-importance, meaning, and purpose to their lives, albeit in a bitter, cynical, and unproductive way. Unfortunately, he used his charm and personality to keep himself busy socially and essentially did nothing else with regard to his job. Much of what is going on could be interpreted as his inability to take responsibility for his own actions by drawing those who trusted him into a potentially job-threatening action. Clearly, he has succeeded in painting the administrative staff as the bad guys here because they actually did something about it. Elaine and Jane need to step away from the emotionality of the situation and try to get a clear perspective before they take any action. They need to ask themselves the following questions:

Can we afford the consequences of Donnie's request should
we be discovered?

If we are discovered, will Donnie step forward in our defense?
Will it matter?

What could be Donnie's motives for asking us to do such a thing?

If this whole thing ends up in court, are we prepared to testify
for Donnie?

Have we really heard both sides of this story?

Have we been fair to Sean and Bob in this matter?

Is Donnie really our friend or could he just be using us?

If Donnie's coworkers were able to see the damage he was doing to the library instead of worrying about his welfare, they might not be so sympathetic, and they certainly would not be willing to risk their own jobs for his sake. But Donnie is a charismatic personality and has a knack of being able to manipulate people to get what he wants—at least most of the time. In this case, he went too far and lost his job, but he is willing to take a few down with him, if necessary. After all, it's not his fault he lost his job; it is always someone else who is out to get him, so he thinks.

Elaine, of course, should not do what Donnie is asking, but how can she be stopped if the administration is not aware of the situation? The director and the supervisor may not be aware that Donnie is continuing to try to play on the staff's sympathies and should take certain precautions with this in mind. For one, paper trails should be carefully assembled, and only pertinent evidence should be retained. Nothing should be kept that is not relevant. Donnie's current state of mind leads him to believe that there is incriminating evidence out there (there may not be anything). Regardless, supervisors should keep scrupulous employee-related records of all contacts regarding this case, not just what is necessary. What Donnie received as his personnel record is all there is—and all there should be. Sloppy or inappropriate record keeping and even e-mail communications have gotten many a corporate mogul in trouble these days—and can get supervisors in trouble too if they don't document personnel actions carefully.

The library administration in this scenario has its hands full with the rebuilding of trust among its staff. However, Elaine and her coworkers should move on and allow Donnie to find his way elsewhere. Above all, they must not allow themselves to be drawn into this inappropriate behavior. Their attempts to help him will only backfire if they try.

SCENARIO 12
This Place Is a Zoo!

Type of Library: Community college library

Area of Library: Reference Department

Greta Vickery wanted to scream. There was that woman and her children again. They were settling in at a public-access computer in front of the reference desk, as they usually did about once a week. And they were there right during the busiest times. The woman looked to be in her late twenties or early thirties. She was bedraggled and had dark circles under her eyes. And it was no surprise, considering her situation: two young children and a baby in a stroller. The older children appeared to be about six and eight years old, and the baby was still nursing. And, of course, everyone knew that, since the woman would breast-feed the child while she was working at the computer! The children ran about the room, climbing on the printers or spreading out on the floor or at a table with their toys or coloring books. They weren't bad kids, but the setting was wrong. The other students at Austin County Community College were patient. After all, most of them were working folks with families of their own. But the situation in the reference room was spiraling out of control, and Greta and her boss, Director Betty Lemons, were at odds on how to deal with it.

Betty believed that the library was for the community and that almost anything could be accommodated. Sure, they were fortunate since they did not have much trouble with street people—the public library had to deal with that all the time. But the college's library facilities were stretched thin. It was not a rich institution, and the six public-access catalogs available were intended for the students and were constantly occupied.

Greta was frustrated when she was not allowed to limit certain types of behavior—Betty would not hear of it. So, day after day, she had to bite her lip when the noise levels mounted higher and higher. Besides the woman and her passel of children, there were the cell phones ringing, the printers grinding out free printing, and the teenagers playing their music devices. Their earphones did not seem to reduce the noise. Greta had finally drawn one line in the sand—no boom boxes were allowed. Greta also wanted to put up a sign stating that the public-access computers were there for scholarly research, but Betty thought that was too restrictive. So, students used the computers to check their e-mail and cruise the Web for goodness knows what. Although Greta supported intellectual freedom in principle, she knew that patrons who were goofing off often thwarted students needing to do real research for their assignments. The other thing that bugged Greta and did not seem to bother Betty was the amount of idle chitchat that was tolerated among the public services staff. There were times when Greta's colleagues would stand at the reference desk talking about whatever they had for lunch yesterday while students were waiting for help. Surely Betty could see that service was suffering!

Was Greta just being old-fashioned? She decided maybe she needed to find another job if things continued this way.

Pat's Assessment

Greta and Betty need to realize that the issues of who uses the library and how they use it are about the mission and policies of the library. Without leadership-level decisions about the library's operating principles, the results are the kind of chaos that Greta, the staff, and their customers (the students, faculty, and general public) experience every day.

To create a strategic plan that really means something will take some time, but it will be worth the effort in the end. Betty should check in with her professional associates for advice. Input from all directions, including staff, faculty, students, and administrators at the community college, will be invaluable. In addition, she should solicit advice from her counterparts at local public and school libraries as well as her colleagues at nearby academic libraries and the general public. Surveys, focus groups, and joint meetings with these groups will give Betty, Greta, and the rest of the staff important insights as to the relationship of the community college library with the rest of the community.

Betty can first work on solving specific problems by determining their causes. For example, she may notice a trend of overcrowding of the library by high school students and the bored younger siblings for whom they are responsible. The local public library and the high school library have inadequate collections for college-bound students, so they have no choice but to use the community college's resources. A solution might be to coordinate resources with the other local libraries and share public relations budgets so that the community can learn that the public library does have the right books and magazines to support high school students and is also equipped to provide programs for the younger brothers and sisters.

While she is addressing these immediate problems, Betty should collaborate with her staff to craft a plan, stating the operating principles of the library and the guidelines for information access and customer behavior. Every staff member must learn courteous ways to set limits while steering patrons to more desirable behaviors. The staff should establish time limits at the computers and other usage rules giving students first choice during certain hours as well as govern the behavior of minors (and adults), with reasonable consequences if rules are ignored or broken.

Glenda's Assessment

PERSPECTIVES

Greta: I wish Betty would do her job! She should have posted rules and ordered everyone to enforce them. It's all her fault, but I'm the one getting migraine headaches! Betty should make up for lost time and correct this situation now!

Betty: I know that Greta is unhappy, but her description of the problem is off base. My philosophy is simply different from hers. I believe that we are here to serve the needs of our public, whoever and whatever they are. For example, the young mother is bringing her children to the library so frequently because she is homeschooling them, and hopefully this will lead them to a lifelong desire to read and learn. There's nothing wrong with that! Today many courses use team-learning approaches, and these students need to have a place to discuss class assignments. It is impossible to do that without making some noise. I am pleased to know that our library is serving these needs so well. I have not received complaints from the other staff members, so I can only assume that the problem is Greta's. Just to be sure, I'll have a one-on-one conference with each staff member to see how the others feel.

I will refer Greta to the employee assistance program so that she can learn to deal with frustrations more effectively. I will also do a needs assessment and evaluation survey to find out the perceptions of the clients. If they suggest a need for more control, I will then enlist my staff to help me work out the problems. If they suggest, for example, that they have to wait for access to the computers, we could then limit computer use to a maximum time for each user. But I will never try to dictate what sites they can access because I believe strongly in unrestricted searching for information.

If the clients are satisfied, then I shall continue to be satisfied, and Greta can find a job elsewhere if she can't adjust to this one.

SUGGESTIONS FROM AN EMPLOYEE ASSISTANCE PERSPECTIVE

This is an example of a common problem of employees who disagree in philosophy with their supervisors and try to force the supervisors to change policies and procedures to agree with their own personal beliefs. Sometimes their attitudes are based on reasonable approaches, and sometimes not. Greta's dissatisfaction is not a sufficient reason for Betty to change anything without additional input. I suggest that Betty conduct periodic assessment and evaluation surveys to find out the perceptions of the clients. If they suggest a need for more control, she should evaluate the rules and see where changes are needed. She should enlist Greta's help in interpreting the results of the surveys so that Greta will not think that Betty distorted the input.

Authors' View

The clash here is not just a philosophy difference between employee and employer; this situation reflects a cultural shift that libraries of most types are experiencing. The quiet, peaceful reading room of the past has been replaced by noisy group work, the din of technology, and constant multi-tasking. Libraries must find ways not only to cope with the change but also embrace it and provide services that reflect it.

It is Betty's job as director to inspire and encourage the staff to get with the program as well as improve the program. Greta is longing for a past that simply does not exist anymore. If Greta cannot adjust, she certainly is in the wrong job. Yet she is right that certain limits could help redirect the chaos. For example, wouldn't it be nice for libraries that cater to working people and families to have child-care areas nearby in the building so that students can safely leave their small children there while they concentrate on their research? Game rooms, listening and viewing rooms, and Internet cafés could be instituted for less serious pursuits, leaving designated areas available for reference searching. Group study areas and individual study areas can be separated to reduce noise problems. Instead of complaining and getting frustrated, Greta would do well to help think of solutions like these that provide the services needed rather than reducing some for the sake of others.

Realistically, some of the ideas suggested here might not be possible financially, but considering them may lead to opportunities to make them

happen. Betty and her staff should work together to come up with ways to meet the needs of their users, under the umbrella of a mission and vision that are relevant for their institution.

SCENARIO 13
The Problem with Eddie

Type of Library: Medium-sized public
Area of Library: Administration and all others

"Bryan, it's happening again." Director Bryan Little knew exactly what was happening as Associate Director Jill Gambee stuck her head into his office that morning. A sense of dread settled over Bryan. Ever since he'd taken the library director's position at Middle Fork Public Library six months ago, he'd found himself facing issues for which neither his PhD program nor his library school degree had prepared him. Such was the one facing him now.

"What are you going to do about it? How can we let him continue?" Jill wanted to know.

Who Jill was referring to was Eddie Mastin, a long-term support staff member with a history of emotional problems. Over the years, Eddie had been passed from department to department in the hopes of finding a "good fit" for his personality. Most of the time, Eddie was a diligent soul who did acceptable work. However, he was given to emotional outbursts, with screaming and yelling, triggered when things did not go his way or he was corrected for some infraction. These incidents were becoming more frequent and his speech and behavior more vitriolic.

The targets of Eddie's wrath were usually female employees. Eddie had once been unhappily married and was now unhappily divorced. He carried his losses like a festering sore, which, if touched in some way, would unleash his fury. Although Eddie had never physically attacked anyone, his verbal fury would send his victim running to the restroom in tears. If the victim yelled back, a screaming match would escalate to the point of sending others in the department racing for cover. Over the years, Eddie's rages had caused more than one individual to request a transfer or even resign.

Eddie's current supervisor, Mary Brown, an elderly woman two years from retirement, refused to intervene and simply withdrew to her office and shut the door.

When Bryan began to examine Eddie's employment files, he found several letters of complaint and appeals for assistance. What he did not find was a record of official documentation regarding Eddie's behavior. All of Eddie's yearly evaluations were uniformly acceptable, and as a result, Eddie had a satisfactory official work record. No one had ever wanted to take on the unenviable task of "belling the cat." Until today, Bryan had let the incidents run their course and tried to let the situation calm itself down. He'd spoken to Eddie twice, outlining how his behavior was unacceptable and asking him to account for himself.

Each time, Eddie had been repentant but indicated that he felt provoked and justified. He promised not to let it happen again and even offered to apologize to his victim.

"I'm coming," Bryan sighed, as he got out of his office chair and headed out toward the fracas. He could hear Eddie yelling and someone else sobbing; all the other staff huddled at their desks looking up at him as he passed by. Jill's words rang in his ear, "What are you going to do?" Bryan really didn't know.

Pat's Assessment

When Bryan came to the library as the new director, there were no sustainable policies for evaluating employees on both technical performance and treatment of other people. He needs to create a culture where people understand that intellectual achievement and technical know-how are not enough, and impressive credentials do not excuse uncivil behavior toward anyone. On the other hand, being nice is not a substitute for productivity. Good work and good manners must go hand in hand with productivity for the library to prosper.

To create this kind of environment over time, Bryan should develop a multitask approach to the issue of how everyone, including administrators, is to be evaluated, coached, and rewarded for what most people would call good behavior. There will naturally be stumbling blocks on the path to excellence—Eddie is one of them.

Bryan's first step will be to organize a workshop to outline expected standards of behavior. In his opening speech he should let the staff know, in word and deed, that certain behaviors would not be acceptable in the library, including yelling, abusive language, and so forth. He must be careful to phrase his concerns in positive terms, talking about how everyone could

work together with respect toward each other and toward library patrons. This is also the time to lay out his long-term plan for improving the work environment and how he is going to involve everyone in the planning and implementation process.

In the first week of his new regime, he should meet with all of the department heads as a group, and then individually, and talk with them about the issues. He needs to let them know that he expects them to manage people, not just systems and items, and that he will assist them in the goal of becoming better communicators.

When the problem with Eddie comes to Bryan's attention, Bryan should warn the department heads about using Eddie as a scapegoat for the institution's inability to deal swiftly with problem behavior. If the department heads do not treat the cause of the problem, even if Eddie leaves, another "Eddie" is waiting to happen. There also is the concern that some of the reports of Eddie's behavior were inflamed and distorted by past events. Bryan should make it clear that all incidents must be recorded fairly and objectively.

With regard to Eddie's own unit, Bryan should outline the following rules:

> Eddie will be evaluated based on future behavior. No more pop psychology discussions about his emotional state, his personal life, and so forth. The department head needs to cease gossiping about Eddie and to turn "Eddie" conversations to different topics unless an actual incident is being discussed. And then, only the person involved should be asked to discuss what happened, privately. He or she would be asked to refrain from discussing it with others, in order not to add fuel to the fire. In other words, Eddie's bad behaviors cannot be allowed to let other people off the hook about their own behaviors.

> Since past administrations had not documented Eddie's problems, it is *illegal* and *unethical* to drag up the past. Everyone starts with a clean slate.

> If Eddie blows up at one of his coworkers again, swift action will be needed on the part of the department heads—Bryan will back them up.

Within two weeks of outlining these rules, Bryan should call another workshop on workplace behavior and what would be expected from employees. This time, Bryan should collaborate with the human resource director to outline the interim procedure for inappropriate behavior. A printed guide-line should be handed to everyone. In every department, a meeting should be held within a week of the workshop to give all employees a chance to give feedback.

Bryan must set the stage by being both good-humored and firm. The first few months of implementing these ideas might be awkward and some-times even a little embarrassing, as well-intended people made mistakes. So he should instruct his staff to cut each other some slack as they learn what works best.

Basically, the workshop should remind people of the guidelines for good behavior and alert staff as to what would happen if they violate these rules. When a specific incident occurs, there would be a private meeting with the people involved, and the supervisor would facilitate a meeting where, in effect, a simple behavior contract would be put in place, with con-sequences. In other words, it does not work to chastise people about their behavior if there is not an agreement about what the right behavior is. There needs to be an agreement about what criteria will be used to make sure things work, follow-up meetings, and meaningful consequences.

Meanwhile, an all-staff committee can be formed to establish a set of evaluation policies. Based on state and national evaluation policies, or those of similar libraries, these policies will be used as a guide by the Middle Fork Public Library to develop its own standards for workplace behavior.

Glenda's Assessment

PERSPECTIVE

Bryan: Supervisor Brown should have documented Eddie's actions and should have considered his actions in preparing Eddie's evaluations over the years—regardless of how old she is or how near retirement! I don't think the problem is entirely Eddie; the problem is also this supervisor!

SUGGESTIONS FROM AN EMPLOYEE ASSISTANCE PERSPECTIVE

Bryan must call in Supervisor Brown and explain to her that one of her re-sponsibilities as a supervisor is to show Eddie the written policies and warn him that any future occurrences will be recorded and can be used as the basis for corrective action. If she does not agree to do this, she can retire two years early! The supervisor can explain that if Eddie receives two warnings

(assuming the policy says something to that effect), he will be at risk of being fired on the third.

Bryan should ask human resources personnel to do a workshop showing supervisors how to document employee behaviors and the importance of providing a fair and accurate evaluation.

When I work with clients, I receive *many* complaints from employees who have never been adequately warned about their misdeeds and have received satisfactory or even outstanding ratings in their annual evaluations. If such is the case, the manager deserves the problem he gets!

This episode should be written up and documented, and the current supervisor must be informed that she is now responsible for handling these situations, and her evaluation will suffer if she fails to do so quickly and appropriately. She should be required to provide Eddie with a letter informing him that he must report to the employee assistance office by a specific date and must participate in counseling and in a formal anger-management curriculum. Failure to do so will result in loss of employment. Further, he should be informed in writing that any subsequent anger episode will result in loss of employment. It is not fair that other employees should have to work in such a threatening environment.

Authors' View

This scenario is a variation on the one with Donnie—although in this case the employee has an explosive temper instead of charismatic charm. Not documenting and not counseling Eddie on his bad behavior and a lack of commitment to uphold civility in the workplace has allowed this problem to reach its current state. One of the worst problems we face in libraries is the lack of acceptable or—in some cases—any management skills on the part of supervisors and administrators. In academic libraries, for example, supervisors are often chosen for unrelated scholarly credentials rather than any demonstrated ability to manage people and resources. The results can be and often are disastrous for the organization. Just because a librarian is a great cataloger or a fabulous reference professional does not mean that the person can manage others. Oftentimes we find colleagues being promoted for the wrong reasons—the classic "Peter Principle." People are not necessarily born with management skills, but these skills can be acquired with proper training, practice, and commitment on the part of the supervisor to be effective in his or her assigned role. Being a supervisor can be a lonely and difficult task. No one enjoys a confrontation with a difficult employee about his or her behavior, but this is a task and a skill that is essential to a healthy workplace. It is also critical that there be established standards of workplace civility that every employee is aware of, with clearly defined consequences for their violation. These standards must cover how conflicts are to be handled and by whom. The standards should also cover how information about the conflict is to be handled. All of this information needs to be communicated to the entire staff. An ideal time to discuss this with employees is when they are hired, during a group meeting, or during a yearly evaluation. Finally, administrators, supervisors, and staff must all commit to taking a role in the promotion of civility in the workplace.

In the end, employees must be held accountable for their behaviors in the workplace, and supervisors and administrators must be held accountable for their roles in the management of that environment.

SCENARIO 14
Totally Incompatible?

Type of Library: School system
Area of Library: Whole system

Lisa Wentworth and Jim Page are colleagues in the Green Lake School System. They are each in charge of school media centers that have similar numbers of students but otherwise are different in many ways. Lisa's school is in a poor area of the system, but Lisa is very dedicated to bringing her students into the twenty-first century in spite of the economic obstacles they face. Jim's school is in an affluent suburban area that typically raises nice sums of private money to supplement the county and state funds that are more or less equal to the funding for Lisa's school. But those extra funds make a huge difference, and Lisa is resentful. She also has a paranoid streak that Jim finds extremely bothersome. Jim believes that Lisa plays up her "underdog" role way too much and in fact spends too much of her time whining. Lisa, on the other hand, believes that Jim has a cavalier attitude because of his privileged status.

The differences in their work environments are aggravated by the fact that Lisa's and Jim's personal habits and political views are also about as different as they could be. Lisa is a left-leaning Democrat, former welfare recipient, and single mother. Jim comes from a conservative background, is independently wealthy from old family money (although he downplays this fact since he knows it might be viewed negatively by his colleagues), and although he is quite committed to public education in principle, he sends his three kids to parochial school.

Lisa and Jim constantly clash in every public and administrative forum where they come in contact. And these meetings are not always in relation to school functions. Both are active in local politics and town functions, so their arguments often go beyond school media issues. Naturally, they are at opposite ends of topics such as Internet filtering, sex education in the schools, censorship, abortion rights, and many other political issues. About all they agree upon is that school media specialists don't get paid enough, but even that is something that means different things to them. Lisa is still struggling to pay off student loans as the only person in her family to make it to college, whereas Jim does his job because of his love for and dedication to education and has rejected plenty of opportunities to make it big in real estate or stocks.

Both Lisa and Jim are bright, dedicated professionals. What would it take to get them on the same page for education?

Pat's Assessment

This situation is bad enough when Lisa and Jim quibble among themselves, but once it comes to a head, Martha Smith, administrator of the local school district, will have to take action.

Consider the following result of Jim and Lisa's feud: Martha had spent weeks coaxing members of the school board for the Green Lake School System to come to a public meeting about library funding at the new high school. She, and other school media specialists in the system, with the able assistance of the public and academic librarians in the region, had put together an interactive demonstration of some of the really cool technology available to schools. In addition, a librarian-storyteller and a group of student pages engaged the audience in role-playing and learning exercises. Parents, students, teachers, library personnel, and the local media packed the auditorium. The school board was visibly impressed.

And then it happened. No one could say afterward who or what exactly triggered the argument concerning the funding of after-school programs affecting working mothers, but within seconds, Lisa and Jim were at it in a loud and very public manner. The language used and demeanor of the argument resulted in embarrassed parents herding their children out the door, and when it was time for the sales pitch—for more funding needed to automate the libraries—half the audience was gone, including most of the school board members. It was bad enough that Lisa and Jim took up valuable time at committee meetings with their ongoing feud, but the expressions on the school board members' faces as the two media specialists slugged it out verbally were priceless—and Martha would have laughed if she hadn't already known the implications. This would damage the image of the library media specialists and the school system for the foreseeable future in a time when community support was critical.

Martha never thought of herself as someone with a temper, but her family later told her that red laser beams shot from her eyes when she cornered the two miscreants on the steps of the high school, where they had carried their argument outside.

"You selfish, stupid children," she screamed. They looked at her in shock. "I don't care who is right and who is wrong. Your anger at each other just blew a major project that your colleagues and students have worked on for weeks. And I will be surprised if the school board votes a dime for your libraries in the next ten years!"

Martha said some other things, some unprintable, and stormed off in tears.

The next day, when cooler heads prevail, Martha should have someone neutral call both Lisa and Jim and ask them to come to a meeting with her to help salvage the situation. A mediation consultant should be asked to participate in discussing the issues, because Martha can no longer remain neutral in this situation. It is important to invite a colleague to support each of the employees involved.

Martha needs to set the tone for a productive meeting and show leadership by first graciously apologizing to Jim and Lisa for her own behavior. She can tell them how hurt she was at their actions and how her anger came from the fear that they had done irreversible damage to the libraries in their area. If Jim and Lisa begin talking at once, defending their behavior, the mediator will interrupt them. It will be critical that he instills in them the importance of listening to the others and responding to the discussion rather than protecting one position or another.

When Lisa and Jim seem to calm down, the mediator should explain the agenda for the afternoon. First, he will need to help Lisa and Jim resolve some of their issues so that they might be able to conduct themselves in a more productive manner in public meetings. Second, he should facilitate a brainstorming session about how to salvage the previous day's disaster.

Though many communication tricks might work here, there is one that can help Lisa and Jim become more sympathetic to the other person's point of view and learn to listen and respond more appropriately. Lisa and Jim should be instructed to interview each other for fifteen minutes and find out why the other person became a school media specialist. Then, both of them will be asked to give a presentation to the rest of the group about what they discovered. This little exercise will force them to listen carefully to what the other person is saying.

Through this exercise, Lisa can learn the depth of Jim's commitment to the children and that he had to pay his own way through school when his parents refused to pay his tuition for what they thought was a demeaning job. Jim can hear about the kind of sacrifices Lisa made for her work and what it was like being a single mom. Jim and Lisa will each present the other's professional biography and personal mission with a new understanding of each other.

The group can then begin the delicate work of deciding how to patch up the situation left over from the prior meeting.

Glenda's Assessment

PERSPECTIVES

Lisa: That jerk should learn to keep his mouth shut! I can't just sit there quietly when he's the one who always starts the name-calling! I can't stand it when he accuses me of whining, especially since he was born with a silver spoon in his mouth. If he only knew how much I have suffered, he'd have some understanding!

I wish Jim's coordinator would just tell him to shut up! There's no way I'm going to let him get by with what he's doing!

Jim: That liberal should learn to keep her mouth shut! I can't just sit there quietly when she's the one who always starts the name-calling! I can't stand to hear the bitch whine, and that's all she ever does. She thinks the whole world should give her everything she wants just because she's had a few bad breaks. Who hasn't?

I wish Lisa's coordinator would just tell her to shut up! There's no way I'm going to let her get by with what she's doing!

SUGGESTIONS FROM AN EMPLOYEE
ASSISTANCE PERSPECTIVE

Martha should talk with these two individuals before any major fund-raising program is launched or there is any meeting with the public or the school board and explain that they can fight quietly in private, but if they do this in public, their jobs are in jeopardy and their evaluations will be affected. Job descriptions should include items that Jim's and Lisa's coordinators can evaluate, such as cooperation, teamwork, and so forth, and their coordinators should be very clear about the fact that teamwork and loyalty are important parts of their work.

Then Martha should call a meeting with Lisa and Jim together to talk about possible ways that they can leave their private and political views out of the equation and work on planning for the good of the entire school system, not just their individual schools.

If some specific need arises (such as a systemwide fund-raising program or public relations program involving the public or school board or both), Martha will pay a mediator to work with them prior to any public exposure. If this doesn't help, she may wish to make their participation in the program dependent upon their commitment to civil behavior.

Martha should write a letter to both explaining that their jobs must be kept separate from personal beliefs that appear to interfere with appropriate functioning. She should inform them that they must sign an agreement stating they understand that they will be held accountable for any further disruption and that if this happens again, they will be required to attend mediation sessions or have their jobs terminated.

Authors' View

This is one of those situations where two adversaries might have become great friends if they had only known each other in a different context. We find conflicts like this one in all walks of life. In the movies, these people end up as lovers or champions of something great. Pat's assessment shows how this can actually happen, even after being committed enemies for a long time.

This is also an issue of the public behavior of professionals. Martha has the right to expect a certain level of civility from those reporting to her while they are together in a public forum or where their actions affect the school district at large. Lisa and Jim have allowed their personal differences to disrupt the organization as a whole. They behaved badly, and now everyone will suffer because of their thoughtlessness and emotional imma-turity. Martha is well within her rights to demand that Lisa and Jim confine their personal beliefs to their private conversations. Martha may wish to help them find a mediator as mentioned above, but Lisa and Jim are not re-quired to like each other or agree on issues. They must, however, conduct themselves as professionals.

We all know of situations like this. One of the problems is the establish-ment of history—once adversaries have established battle lines and both have allies and victories behind them, it is hard to come to a truce, much less a meeting of the minds.

However, once in a while an issue arises that unites even the most bitter of enemies. It is at times like this that the opportunity to mediate becomes powerful. Mediation services need more prominence in our institutions.

Mediation is, simply, "any process for resolving disputes in which another person helps the parties negotiate a settlement" (Beer and Stief 1997, 3). Although it can be much more than that, mediation is a popular and suc-cessful method for resolving conflicts that arise from personal differences. Long-standing workplace conflicts that fit this profile may be candidates for mediation. Certainly, "mediation is useful in a wide variety of conflicts" (3). Furthermore, mediation is often useful in the "aftermath of an incident, at the point when emotions have eased enough that the parties can begin to negotiate" (3).

We recommend Jennifer E. Beer and Eileen Stief's book, *The Mediator's Handbook*, for more information on this process. Many institutions and or-ganizations have adopted such mediation processes to defuse personnel ac-tions that have the potential to spiral out of control, drawing the victims into a legal morass that has no end in sight.

SCENARIO 15
Is It Really All That Important?

Type of Library: Urban public school media center

Area of Library: Technology Support

Marietta Rhodes had been a media specialist at Carver Senior High School for about a year. She settled into her new position as assistant librarian for technology at the urban high school, and she enjoyed working with students and got along well with her fellow teachers and library colleagues. It was a challenge to meet the technology needs of a public school with a budget stretched in so many directions, and the school had all the typical problems one would expect in an urban setting. In spite of it all, Marietta could tell she was making a difference.

"Hi, Marietta, could you call Evan out here for us?" asked Allan Chatham, one of the more senior science teachers at the school, while a group of students from his introduction to biology class milled around nearby. Marietta recognized Allan but had not had an opportunity to work with his classes. Evan Rogers, the head librarian, was at a meeting all day, so Marietta was in charge.

"Evan's out today, but I'm sure I could assist you or at least take a message. What do you need?" Marietta inquired pleasantly.

"I want to set up the lab with some new software I was able to get on state contract for instructional purposes so my biology students can use it with some of their homework assignments. It's got great simulation features for dissection exercises, and so many students nowadays are beyond squeamish about dissection—they think it's an ethical issue! I think it's just an excuse not to have to touch slimy dead frogs, myself."

Marietta had to smile. She had always detested that part of biology herself, so she sympathized. But she had to ask some questions before installing the software.

"OK, then. Do you have a copy of the license agreement or some other documentation authorizing us to load this software on our networked PCs?"

Allan seemed stunned. "What are you talking about? This stuff is on state contract, and we're allowed to use it freely."

"That may be so," Marietta replied evenly. "I'm sure if that's the case there is some kind of release form that comes with the copy of the software you obtained. Did you happen to see that?"

Allan did not seem to understand this question and started shaking his head as though quite confused.

Marietta did not want to appear to be a bureaucrat. But she knew that some longtime teachers, especially those who were not as familiar with the use of software, did not understand how licensing and permissions worked. Fortunately, it usually was just a matter of getting the paperwork in order. "Look, I'm just trying to help. We've got to have that form on file, and I'm sure it won't be complicated to get it if it's on a state contract."

"Maybe I should wait until Evan comes back tomorrow," Allan replied impatiently. "He'd be able to take care of this pronto."

"Evan delegates most of these kinds of issues to me," Marietta explained. "If you could check and see if you have that form—it's not a big deal, really; we just need to have it on file. We do it all the time, you know. In fact, the library is the department that usually obtains the software for classes."

"Maybe you do," Allan replied tersely. "In fact, I'm sure you do," he repeated with sarcasm in his voice. "Just because you're black you think you can jerk me around! Well, we'll see about that," and he turned abruptly and headed out the door of the media center. The students looked at each other in confusion and trailed after him.

Marietta stood there with her mouth hanging open. Did he think she'd gotten her job because of her race? How was she supposed to react? She'd talk to Evan tomorrow. Maybe it wasn't all that important. Maybe Allan was just having a bad day. She knew the issue was really about the software—the media center usually handled the licenses for state contract software, so Allan was out of line and confused about procedure, but that could be taken care of. It was the personal attack that really bothered her. All she knew was she felt less than human right now and wanted to just go home and climb into bed with a hot cup of tea. She had not been treated this badly so openly in a long time, and she hated how it made her feel. It brought back bad memories, and she knew she would not sleep that night.

Pat's Assessment

Marietta needs to go to Evan immediately and explain what happened. Evan should explain to Marietta the school district's policies for inappropriate behavior between staff members, particularly when students are present. Consequently, there will need to be an official investigation. There are two issues here. First, there was the issue of Allan using race, which triggered important legal and ethical issues. Second, there was the problem of the students. Allan's words would have wounded anyone in range as well as send a message to the students that such behavior was acceptable. Evan will need to take immediate steps.

First, Evan should alert the principal. The principal should take over, scheduling a meeting with Allan and giving him a chance to explain his behavior. The principal should meet with Allan, Marietta, Evan, and Jill, the head of the science department. (Since the perception of fairness is very important, Jill's presence would lend moral support to Allan, just as Evan would be there to stand by Marietta.)

By this time, the school is likely buzzing with rumors about the big blowup in the library, and a few parents have no doubt called wanting to know what had happened. Staff should be instructed to be vague with the details, telling parents that it was a disagreement between two teachers and that it was being dealt with.

When the four colleagues meet, Marietta and Allan should have the opportunity to discuss the incident directly. They are likely to be uneasy at first, but this will help identify the causes of Allan's outburst. In this case, Allan was embarrassed when Marietta seemed to correct him in front of the students, so he lashed out. Allan should take this opportunity to apologize for his behavior, and Marietta can express that she is ready to make her peace and move on.

If all parties can agree to put the incident behind them, the principal should issue a brief report to human resources and the Equal Employment Opportunity Commission officer that there had been a misunderstanding between Allan and Marietta and it had been resolved. The parties should also agree to keep discussion of the incident to a minimum. Most likely, the incident will blow over.

Next, Allan will need to do some damage control to minimize the effects of the incident on the students who saw and heard it. With Marietta present, Allan should tell the students that he had made a mistake and publicly apologize to Marietta. A guided discussion about manners and civility might follow.

If all parties involved are able to remain levelheaded, the climate in the library should return to normal. Allan is likely to avoid the library, and Marietta may avoid talking to Allan at meetings, but even with coolness between the two, they should be able to maintain a professional relationship.

Glenda's Assessment

PERSPECTIVES

Marietta: I don't know whether he meant it as a racial slur or not, but he did throw in the word *black* in an ugly tone. I'll tell Evan about it and hope he handles it correctly, but what if he gives in? We are obviously required by copyright laws to follow the license agreement, and Evan has been very good about that, but I worry this time! So far, I've trusted Evan, but my trust could be lost on this one.

Evan: Marietta is one of the most competent librarians I've ever known, and I deeply regret that this happened. But how can I appease this patriarchal teacher who has been here so long? So far, we have been able to comply with copyright laws, and I don't want to start backsliding now, but how shall I handle this? I know the "correct" answer, but I hate to be put in the middle. If I make an exception, Marietta will think I've let her down and that I've given in to a racist attitude. But if I say no to Allan, he'll spread the word throughout the staff that they can't depend on me to support them.

SUGGESTIONS FROM AN EMPLOYEE ASSISTANCE PERSPECTIVE

Evan must not give in to Allan despite his fears about the word spreading. Two factors are important here: obeying the law and establishing an appropriate work environment for his staff member. Therefore, he must, in as gentle a way as possible, offer to assist Allan in getting the necessary documentation. He might even take personal responsibility for his failure to inform the entire staff of the regulation and apologize to both Allan and Marietta. In dealing on a personal level with Marietta, he might suggest to her that her concerns are legitimate and that she might benefit from a session or two with the employee assistance counselor to deal with her personal feelings about racism and inappropriate treatment by colleagues. This kind of treatment can add considerably to the stress levels of mistreated individuals, and counseling can help with these effects.

Authors' View

Sometimes a conflict is not what is seems. In this particular scenario, racism may or may not be an issue. It's important in such exchanges not to blow things out of proportion. We can never know exactly what someone is thinking, but we can address what he or she does. When people blurt out words without thinking, such as calling each other names, yelling, and so forth, it is most important to act swiftly while treating all parties with respect.

It would have been ideal if Evan had introduced Marietta more thoroughly to all the teachers prior to the beginning of the school year. But in reality, we often do not have time to anticipate all the possible bumps in the road, and even if we know what they are, it is not always possible to cover them. So Marietta was on her own with Allan. But Marietta has had plenty of time to figure out which teachers might be problems—in various ways. Allan has a problem with technology—and with the rules regarding it—and his embarrassment about these issues led to an inappropriate outburst. Such interactions are not uncommon in the workplace.

Quick intervention, honest communication, and the ability to say "I'm sorry" can go a long way in such instances. Keeping the incident low to the ground and not inflaming the situation is important. Sensitivity to all individuals' parts in the drama is also key. And acknowledging that "otherness" can be manifested in many ways and can bring out fear unexpectedly is also invaluable. Today's workplace is changing rapidly, and yet sometimes a misunderstanding is essentially about a policy—not a person's race, gender, sexual orientation, or cultural distinction. We have a tendency to fall back on stereotypes when confronted with a frustrating situation.

Seniority gives no one the right to be rude, though such behavior is often tolerated. It's important for new members of a library staff (no matter what kind of library) to receive orientation that allows them an understanding of the people with whom they will be working and gives them information to help them do their jobs well and help others to do theirs too. This often does not happen—sometimes simply because no one thinks of it or it's perceived that no one has time to do an orientation. This can lead to many misunderstandings that would have been easily avoided. Take the time to get to know your coworkers if you are new. Take time to get to know the new hires if you have been around a while. Regardless of everything else, making this first step in either direction can ultimately make a huge difference in how everyone gets along.

SCENARIO 16
Thou Shalt Not Suffer . . .

Type of Library: Urban public library

Area of Library: Children's Department

Melissa Richardson was pleased with her new position as children's librarian at the Rockland Heights Public Library branch in the large eastern urban center she'd recently come to call home. It was quite a change from the slow-paced, Pacific Northwest small-town environment she'd come from, but she liked the busy, diverse atmosphere. She enjoyed working with the people who came to the library and especially with the children during story hour. Her supervisor, the library's branch manager, Ed Griffin, was a soft-spoken older gentleman, only a few years from retirement.

One Friday morning during a staff meeting, Melissa was asked to hand out a series of forms needed by the city for insurance purposes. As Melissa leaned over to pick up the stack of forms, Gina Overby, the circulation librarian, spied the pendant Melissa always wore around her neck as it slipped from her blouse into plain view of the group.

"What's that?" Gina asked. "It looks like a star. Are you Jewish?"

"It's a pentagram," Melissa replied, blushing as she stuffed it back into her blouse.

"What does it mean? Why do you wear it?" Gina persisted.

"It's a religious symbol," Melissa answered, dreading the possible impact of the words that came next. "You see, Gina, I am a Wiccan."

"You mean you're a witch?" Elaine Morrison from cataloging interjected. "Oh, dear God in heaven!"

Melissa blushed as she tried to explain that Wiccans are those who worship the divine as inherent in nature.

"You mean you go around casting spells and worshiping and sexually consorting with the devil!" Elaine said loudly. "That's what my preacher says Wiccans do! How could you do such things?"

"All right, all right, that's enough of this talk," said Ed, trying to regain control of a routine meeting gone haywire.

Silence fell over the room as he went over the instructions for filling out the forms and dismissed the meeting. As the staff members were filing out, Ed said, "Melissa, I need to see you in my office at 2:00 this afternoon."

Melissa nodded and took the back hallway to her office. After what seemed like an eternity, she knocked at Ed's door.

"Have a seat, Melissa," Ed said. "We have to decide what to do about this witchcraft thing. Why do you wear that necklace to work?"

"I'm sorry," Melissa stammered, "but I've done nothing wrong. I've never pushed my beliefs or even mentioned them to anyone here at the library. This is a big metropolitan area; I chose to move here because there was a community that supported my beliefs. I have a right to worship as I please, I harm no one, and it's not really anybody's business. Besides, my rapport with the public is great, the children love me, and I don't see what the problem is or why we have to do anything. I believe I am entitled by the Constitution to freedom of religion."

"Personally, Melissa," Ed said, "I don't care what you believe or do on your time off so long as it doesn't affect our branch in a negative manner. We've worked for a long time to build the library's relationship with this part of the city, and I don't intend to risk our future over this issue. The main office is thinking about closing branches, you know."

"Also, in case you haven't noticed, Melissa, this is a tightly knit, conservative neighborhood with traditional values. Elaine Morrison is highly respected here, and you can bet that within a week everyone within a radius of twenty blocks will know a witch works here. This could bring the veritable wrath of God, so to speak, down on this branch and on your head as well. I'm sorry, Melissa, but until this mess blows over, I am relieving you of story time and any further contact with children and am assigning you to work back in book return processing. It's for your own good, believe me."

"Please don't do this," Melissa said through her tears. "I haven't done anything wrong."

"Look, it's Friday, and you are not scheduled to work this weekend, right?" Ed asked. "Let me think this over, but for now, report to book return processing on Monday."

Melissa left the office, cried in the bathroom, and then walked slowly back to her office. To her dismay, when she returned to her desk, it was covered with Bible tracts. She tossed them into the trash and tried to go through the motions of work until the day ended.

When she returned to work the next Monday, she found she was persona non grata. No one spoke to her except in measured, impersonal tones as she processed returned circulated items in the back room. No one invited her to go on coffee break or to lunch as they had before. She decided to bear the isolation and try to rise above the situation, although her sense of despair deepened as the week progressed. Each day she found religious tracts on her desk or in her chair, along with unsigned notes indicating that her soul was doomed. The final straw came when she found a note on her desk that read, "Thou shall not suffer a witch to live!"

Melissa stared at it, realizing that the note could only have come from someone on the staff. Melissa thought incredulously, "Is my life in danger? Who can I trust? What should I do?" When she left that evening, as she started to get into her car, she gazed down and to her horror discovered her left rear tire had been slashed. And someone had scrawled the word witch on the driver's side door in permanent marker.

Pat's Assessment

The tire-slashing incident should be the trigger for Melissa to report the harassment to her supervisor. Ed's initial reaction (making Melissa work in backroom book returns) seems to have been based on his own fears, and after thinking about it carefully, he will have to use his authority as the head of the branch to set the tone of how people treat each other. The rules of the library system are pretty clear about the difference between civil and uncivil behavior, and Ed has to make a stand.

After Elaine's first remarks to Melissa, Ed should have initiated the following conversation:

> "Elaine," he said, "I need to remind you that in this workplace we have some important rules about how we treat each other. They are to protect you, me, Melissa, and every other employee from feeling fearful and attacked. Elaine, you have strong views about your religious practices, and the rules protect your right to have those practices—as does the Constitution of the United States and of our state. You are not allowed to be attacked verbally by other people, and I can't let you attack others."
>
> "But my religious beliefs are just as valid as hers, and mine say that she is evil," Elaine insisted.
>
> "In the same way our library is a sanctuary for books with different ideas, we need to be a sanctuary for staff and customers with different ideas," Ed replied. "So, Elaine, although I don't expect you to change your views, you need to apologize to Melissa for your outburst. And no one should be trying to change Melissa's views or harassing her about them in any way. After all, she is not trying to change yours, is she?"
>
> Elaine grudgingly agreed that was the case.
>
> "Furthermore," Ed continued, "Melissa is being harassed in ways that could be criminally prosecuted if the perpetrators are discovered. Destruction of personal property and life threats are no laughing matter. Of course, Elaine, I am confident that you have no knowledge of such acts; am I correct?" He looked hard at Elaine as he said this. Elaine turned pale and stammered something that sounded like, "Of course not!"

Next, Ed will have to speak privately with Melissa and assure her that any further incidents of harassment will be dealt with strictly. Of course, the problem is not completely solved, as he and Melissa well know.

Ed might start by saying, "Melissa, I have learned the hard way that our library needs to act forcefully and immediately on issues like this. Whether it is a library customer who calls a staff member a bad name or a staff member who explodes at a colleague, we can't tolerate abusive behavior. If we don't act quickly and decisively, it gives the message that we don't care or, worse, that we tolerate this kind of behavior. Now, as to your Wiccan beliefs, I am going to ask you to make a short, formal presentation about your beliefs to the whole staff as part of the next staff meeting. Can you do it?"

Melissa may become defensive. After all, she should not have to defend her beliefs and may not feel comfortable drawing even more attention to herself.

Ed cannot order Melissa to make a presentation, but he can make the case that educating her coworkers would be an effective method for eliminating prejudice. He should let her know that he will stand behind her and also request that Melissa report all further incidents immediately.

At the all-staff meeting, after Melissa talks about being a Wiccan and answers some questions, Ed should review the rules on civil behavior and the consequences of breaking the rules. He should make it clear that any kind of political or religious proselytizing is against library rules and against the law and that any further incidents will trigger an investigation and appropriate disciplinary action.

With Ed's coaching, it is hoped that Elaine and Melissa will be able to work together civilly. Pretty soon, the staff will find something else to gossip about.

Glenda's Assessment

PERSPECTIVES

Melissa: I have every right to wear this jewelry and practice my faith without harassment! Why are these people so close-minded? They are basing their attacks on false information, and educated people should never do that! They should find out the facts and respect the faith of other people. I was being quiet about my faith, minding my own business. They have no right to treat me like this! I can't decide whether to sue or not, but I would be within my rights to sue!

Ed should make those people stop the harassment and let me do my job. I can't believe he's punishing me when he's the one who is not taking care of the situation. He knows I'm effective with those kids! How dare he put me in the back room doing busywork! I wonder what would happen if I sued Ed . . .

Elaine: I talked with my minister about this, and we agreed to start a prayer campaign to ask God to protect our innocent children from such evil. In the past, I respected Melissa and found her likable, but it is clear that Satan conceals himself in attractive ways; otherwise, he wouldn't fool anybody. So we must watch out for his clever disguises and make sure they don't influence impressionable young people. I am also praying for Melissa, hoping that God can help her to eliminate this evil from her life so that she can become a true Christian. There's no chance that she can have eternal life if she doesn't accept Christ, and God's grace is the only way to avoid eternal damnation!

Thank God that Ed has put Melissa out of sight so that she won't influence innocent children. I hope he realizes that her kind of evil doesn't belong here and that he fires her! I pray that God will give him the strength to stick to the true course!

SUGGESTIONS FROM AN EMPLOYEE ASSISTANCE PERSPECTIVE

Ed should apologize to Melissa and return her to her previous job, making sure that he takes more time to make decisions in the future. He should then set up a meeting with Melissa and Elaine and explain that personal religious beliefs are not to be aired on the job. Further, there must be no religious literature placed on anyone's desk. In the interest of harmony, he might request that both women avoid spreading gossip about the situation. He needs to explain that threats and vandalism are illegal and will be reported to the police.

Since Elaine is a librarian and therefore expected to seek knowledge from appropriate sources, it might be helpful if he suggested to Elaine that she find appropriate literature explaining Wiccan beliefs and practices and that she be prepared to discuss this material in a staff meeting.

Melissa has clearly been wronged and may need supportive counseling from the employee assistance office. Ed should present this possibility, not as Melissa's mental health "problem" but rather as a way of dealing with well-justified feelings that resulted from mistreatment by colleagues and also by Ed himself.

Authors' View

Of all the scenarios we devised, this one caused the most discussion among the authors and their consultants. Clashing religious beliefs can lead to volatile and irresolvable conflict. This is certainly not just a problem in the workplace, as world events make obvious. Sadly, American society, although founded somewhat on the desire for freedom of religious expression, has a long and tragic history of religious intolerance and persecution of religious minorities dating from colonial times to the present day. In several recent cases, people with nonmainstream religious beliefs have found themselves intimidated at work, harassed at home, and even driven from their jobs and communities. In the workplace, it is critical for a supervisor to set the standard of behavior in such cases, regardless of his or her personal religious convictions. Each supervisor needs to take stock of his or her own feelings and long-held perceptions about such issues and develop a public response in keeping with the policies of the parent institution. Melissa, in this case, could have just as easily been a Unitarian-Universalist, Mormon, Muslim, Buddhist, Hindu, or Jew. Her Wiccan beliefs are not the issue, nor is anyone else's beliefs about her choice of spiritual tradition. This is a case, once again, of appropriate workplace behavior. In point of fact, many such belief systems—including Wicca—have legal status as religions and are protected under our Constitution.

Melissa, however, will have to be careful how she responds to this situation as well. She will need to examine her own religious attitudes and perceptions as well as seek personal and legal advice from people and organizations that have established guidelines for individuals who may find themselves harassed for their religious beliefs. The Internet is an excellent place to find such information. Melissa, despite her attempts to communicate her beliefs and friendly behavior, may eventually find herself isolated and the victim of a group ostracism. The sad fact is that the rest of her workdays at the library may become a lonely, painful time for her regardless of her personal attitudes and behaviors and the support she receives from her supervisor. She may eventually have to assess her own personal and professional needs for the future and move on if necessary.

Issues regarding religious beliefs can also present themselves with student employees, who come to our society from other countries and may encounter intolerance of their differing religious traditions. Many academic institutions are taking a proactive stance to these sensitive and politically volatile situations by conducting educational sessions that present the institution's policy regarding the presence, practice, and promotion of religion in the workplace. These sessions provide the opportunity for people to express their concerns, learn about other religious traditions, and, most importantly, understand the boundaries of appropriate workplace behavior. Tolerance of personal and religious differences and the expectation of civil behavior in the workplace must be supported and modeled by management for people from different walks of life to work together successfully. Ed may have waffled at first but rose to the occasion. Not all managers do so well—and often managers suffer dire consequences. If a lawsuit is not a result, at the very least there may be ruined careers or bitter recriminations. Or even violence, unfortunately.

The slashing of a tire and a threat to life are both serious and criminal. This goes beyond simple harassment. Ed's words of warning to Elaine may not have been enough to stop it—and in such cases, the police may have to get involved. It is important to derail the escalation of fear and misunderstanding. Asking Melissa to discuss her religious beliefs in an educational fashion was a brave move. Although in this case it helped, if not handled well, such an attempt at education might only make things worse. Melissa clearly was not interested in proselytizing. However, in some communities where there are several religious groups at odds, the other groups may then demand equal time and may be more aggressive with their pitch.

The best policy is one of openness and tolerance. The very reason our country has laws protecting our freedom of religious expression is so that our differences can coexist peacefully. Libraries should be the first place one would expect to find this principle flourishing. Extending simple human kindness, courtesy, and respect should not violate anyone's belief system.

SCENARIO 17
It's Happening Again . . .

Type of Library: Special library (pharmaceutical company)

Area of Library: Information Center staff and clients

Tina Crenshaw, the Metters Pharmaceutical's Information Center administrative assistant, poked her head into head librarian Dave Feinstein's office one day shortly after lunch.

"Oh, Dave," she called in. "It's happened again. But this time you're going to have to really do something! Kathleen has passed out in the staff lounge, and she's supposed to be conducting a research session with Carl Bickley's chemist team in fifteen minutes. We've got to do something!"

Dave froze in the middle of a bite of tuna-fish salad. Eating lunch in his office was a fairly common occurrence because of the overload of his administrative responsibilities. There were days when he barely had time to breathe. But Kathleen Fussell's substance abuse problems were getting out of hand.

"OK," he sighed. "Let's go roust her. May we can pour some coffee into her and kick her alert enough to deal with the session. Is Ginger here today?" Dave was referring to the part-time research assistant who helped out sometimes in the Information Center. "We could certainly use her to help with that session right now."

"I can go check with Tonya, the processing specialist," Tina replied. "I'll go do that while you deal with Kathleen."

Dave got up and headed for the staff lounge. His heart was heavy. Kathleen had been a dedicated member of the research staff for a long time; her descent into addiction was a slow process that at first had seemed so innocent and so understandable that they all made excuses for her and denied there was a problem. He knew that the whole staff was "enabling" her and covering for her mistakes, not setting consequences for her missed deadlines, and talking about her problem endlessly among themselves instead of doing anything about it. It was time to confront the situation. And this was such irony, considering they worked for a drug company!

Dave spied Kathleen slumped over in one of the easy chairs in the corner; the lounge wasn't occupied just then since all of the researchers were in their labs after lunch, and none had drifted back in for the afternoon break before the end of the workday. But it wouldn't be long until someone showed up.

Dave shook Kathleen's shoulder gingerly. "Kathleen, are you OK? Can you wake up now?" Kathleen flinched and sat up with a start. "What! What is it? I'm OK, really, not a problem!" She seemed disoriented and not completely coherent.

Dave pulled over a chair and sat in it in front of Kathleen. He looked straight at her, his eyes sad. She was having a hard time focusing, but she seemed to know who he was. "Kathleen, this can't go on any longer."

There was a pause as Kathleen continued to shake the haze off. She sighed heavily. Finally, in a small voice, she whispered, "I know."

Dave considered his options as he spoke. This was not the first time they had had a conversation about her "problem." When Kathleen was sober, she was an energetic and creative research librarian whom the scientists appreciated because of her dedication to the search for new information. But in the last two years, there had been a remarkable change in her behavior. She had been through a bitter divorce, but the details were not well known to Dave. Substance abuse had been central to the split, that much he knew.

At any rate, he knew that Kathleen's work performance was slipping badly and that this year at annual review time, the decline could not go undocumented. For the moment, he needed to get her up and going. Otherwise, the research team would miss their appointment—not that such meetings hadn't had to be rescheduled before, but it was becoming all too common.

"Look, Dave," Kathleen began, beseechingly. "I know you think I'm a lush or something. That's not it at all. I'm on painkillers, and they make me sleepy. I think maybe they're not working so well. All I want to do is sleep all the time, but I still feel terrible."

"Kathleen, are you mixing pills with booze?"

She shook her head, although not necessarily in a way that convinced Dave that she was denying it. It seemed she was simply trying to wake herself up.

She smiled in a wry, offbeat way. "Well, what a concept."

Dave was feeling very uncomfortable about this confrontation. He knew that Kathleen was in no condition to meet the group, nor was she in any shape to drive home. He cringed at the thought of sending her home.

"I'll tell you what—why don't we brew up a decent pot of coffee and try to wake you up. In the meantime I'll call Tracy from the corporate health clinic and have her come sit with you until you feel awake enough to go home. It's clear that you aren't going to be able to meet your afternoon session with Carl's team—either Ginger will pitch in or we'll reschedule."

"Argh! I completely forgot about that," Kathleen moaned. "I thought I was going to have the afternoon to work on online search requests. I guess I forgot to put that on my calendar. What a stupid slipup!"

"Well, Kathleen, it's becoming a trend. Can't we get you some help?"

"Dave, I'll be fine, I promise!" Kathleen insisted.

Not this time, Dave thought. Something has to change and soon.

Pat's Assessment

Kathleen's problem is cumulative. Dave started to notice Kathleen's behavior changes about a month after a research team first complained about a missed deadline. First, there were her extended weekends—Fridays stopped at noon, and Mondays did not begin until 1:00 p.m. or later. Then, he noticed the change in her attitude toward deadlines. Instead of being the steady, reliable worker she had always been, she seemed to be on a roller coaster. First, a slump would last for days, and then she would frenetically catch up for a week or more, always giving more than what the jobs required and making a big show of what she had done.

There had been other warning signs too. Her attitude toward her colleagues changed; her crisp fashion statement, formerly a point of pride was deteriorating; and her erratic behavior during meetings could no longer be ignored.

When Dave speaks with Kathleen, he does not have to air his suspicions about her drinking but rather point out the evidence that Kathleen was slipping in several areas, that some of these issues had come up during her last review, and that things were getting worse, not better. Although Kathleen's actions had all of the classic signs of substance abuse, they could also be the result of illness or stress. Dave's concern is her performance at work; he does not need to pry into her personal life.

If Kathleen is indeed dealing with substance abuse, she will likely have a host of excuses. She may also become belligerent and weepy when Dave confronts her, but Dave will have to remain calm and unemotional. He should give her a specific deadline for change and specific areas for improvement. He might set a meeting time for two weeks later to evaluate her improvement in regard to deadlines, hours, and meetings—simple, tangible performance issues that are easy to track and hard to debate.

If by the next meeting Kathleen's behavior has not improved, Dave will need to go for help. He should contact the Human Resources Department, discuss his suspicions, and ask for advice. The HR head will advise Dave to make sure that he is applying the same standards of behavior to Kathleen as to the rest of the staff and to put a lid on the gossip: no character assassination, no hostile work environment—just the facts of her workplace behavior as they affect productivity and her treatment of other people.

Dave should discreetly alert his senior staff not to cover for Kathleen and not to discuss the issue with coworkers. Instead, they should document Kathleen's behavior fairly.

Once he reviews the written documentation provided by his senior staff, Dave can evaluate the gravity of the situation and decide how to act. When he confronts Kathleen with the documented mistakes, someone from HR should be there to witness the meeting and to make sure Kathleen's workplace rights are not violated. If Kathleen becomes emotional, Dave should keep the discussion to the evidence at hand—her performance at work.

In the best-case scenario, Kathleen will respond to the confrontation by taking a leave of absence, deciding to confront her substance abuse (the risk of losing her job sobered her up quickly), and coming back with a forthright confession of her problems and a proposed treatment plan. Dave can support her by adjusting her schedule to allow for AA meetings and therapy. He should protect the rest of his staff by reassigning them so that Kathleen is not supervising anyone until she recovers.

If Kathleen does not admit her problem and commit herself to improvement, Dave will have to fire her, citing her well-documented performance issues. Though he can try to help her, if Kathleen's behavior does not improve, Dave's main responsibility is to protect the rest of his staff and maintain a healthy workplace.

Glenda's Assessment

PERSPECTIVES

Kathleen: How humiliating! How dare he put me in a taxi right there in broad daylight in front of everybody? I was OK—just resting my eyes before going into that meeting. Does he have no sympathy for the effects of pain and the medicine it requires? I'm sure I'm now the laughingstock of the whole staff! I'll call a lawyer and see if I can sue Dave!

Dave: I just got word that Kathleen has passed out again. How embarrassing! I called the employee assistance program addictions specialist, who gave me some ideas about handling this. For one thing, he suggested that I avoid confronting her while she's under the influence. So I didn't talk with her at all. I simply called a taxi and helped her into it, instructing her to go home. I plan to call her to schedule an appointment when she's sober. It's fortunate that I can get Ginger to fill in for her at the last minute, but that's the best I can do. Kathleen didn't like being herded into the cab, but she didn't make much of a scene, and I gave the address to the driver in case she passed out on the way.

SUGGESTIONS FROM AN EMPLOYEE
ASSISTANCE PERSPECTIVE

Kathleen's work performance—not her addiction—is the heart of the problem. Dave should talk with human resources and create a plan for dealing with Kathleen if further incidents occur. Dave should schedule an appointment with Kathleen within the next two days and lay out the plan. To keep her job, Kathleen must agree to enter a treatment center, after which she will agree to follow-up care by the employee assistance program for six months. Kathleen should be required to sign a formal contract outlining those two conditions of probation. If she does not agree to it, she must tender her resignation.

Authors' View

This is another one of those common situations that is often not dealt with until it is already out of control. This is because an employee can have many ways to hide substance abuse from others in the workplace; when it starts to become obvious, it is usually already a serious impediment to the person's life functions. On the other hand, some people can maintain a drug habit or an alcohol problem for years without detection. In such cases, a life-changing event (divorce, death in the family, etc.) may suddenly worsen the problem and bring it to the fore. Another common scenario is for work performance to be consistently below par but not enough to take steps toward firing the person. The hidden nature of such problems is part of why they are so hard to address. The abuser is usually doing everything possible to either hide or deny the problem, and coworkers often assist with this, either purposely or unintentionally.

If as a supervisor you suspect that an employee's poor work performance is linked to substance abuse, you should consult a substance abuse counselor or specialist within your Human Resources Department before confronting the employee. Since addiction is considered a medical condition, the employee has certain legal rights and does not have to discuss such conditions with you. However, you are within your bounds to discuss work performance issues, and you can suggest to the employee that he or she seek assistance for whatever may be causing the failure in work performance. Furthermore, if you actually have evidence that the employee has been using drugs or alcohol in the workplace, you should definitely document this since such behavior is clearly out of bounds in most workplaces. This includes returning to work from break or lunch in an impaired state.

A confrontation regarding substance abuse may take the form of a person-to-person employee counseling session that is kept private, including any notes kept as a result of the discussions. Treat the person with respect and avoid showing your anger or frustration. Keep the focus on the work performance or the particular incident or series of incidents that precipitated the session. Your presentation of the issue should be calm and nonjudgmental. This may be difficult if you have experienced substance abuse in your personal life or in your family or friends. Either way, plan what you're going to say and monitor your own internal dialogues before, during, and after the encounter. You should also be ready for a wide range of responses when the topic is broached. Responses may vary from acknowledgment of the problem, to denial of the problem, to rationalizations for the behavior, to an emotional outburst involving tears or threats against you or the institution. Remain calm and focused throughout this process and do not allow yourself to be drawn into an emotional exchange. If substance abuse is acknowledged, be ready to proceed with recommendations for treatment or referral. It is best to take the posture of assuring the person that you are supportive of his or her efforts to seek treatment and that you have every confidence in his or her ability to recover.

If the individual resists or denies the situation, be ready to refocus on the work performance issues and establish a deadline for improvement or disciplinary action. Do not, under any circumstance, allow yourself to be drawn into a situation where there are no consequences for the person's actions. Some individuals with long-term substance-abuse problems are very clever at manipulating your sympathies and compassion to their benefit. It is a component of the disease. Failure to establish clear boundaries and consequences can draw you and your organization into a cycle of attempt/failure/forgiveness that will be very difficult to ever resolve and set you up for emotional blackmail. You must, as a supervisor, remain firm in your resolve. You owe it to yourself, your colleagues, your staff, and the person with the problem.

If you do not have actual proof of substance abuse, do not bring your suspicions into the conversation. Try to allow the person enough personal sense of trust to reveal the issue to you. However, if the person appears visibly intoxicated, you must not immediately assume that there is a problem with substance abuse. The individual could be on some form of medication he or she is not used to, may be having a reaction, or could be having a medical emergency of some sort. Do not make assumptions until you know exactly what is happening. The central questions are: Is this person capable of performing his or her duties as assigned? Is this person a threat to himself or herself or to others in terms of safety or a disruptive influence to the workplace? If the person is clearly incapacitated, and unable to remain at work, it is probably best to send them home or to a doctor's care. Do not, however, allow them to drive themselves.

In some circumstances, a group confrontation involving other peers and even members of the individual's family can be the way to deal with this problem. However, this procedure, called an intervention, must involve thorough investigation, planning, and the agreement of all involved. Please consult your institutional legal counsel before taking this approach.

Finally, don't ignore this problem and simply hope it goes away; it won't. Seek appropriate assistance from trained professionals, but do not try to play therapist; it is the supervisor's responsibility to see that employees have the resources they need to do their jobs, but it is not the supervisor's place to solve employees' personal problems.

PART THREE

Managing Conflict before It Manages You

Now that we've presented a number of case studies that draw upon what really happens in libraries, our final step is to offer some constructive tools for dealing with conflict. One of the most powerful management movements of the day concerns the concept of emotional intelligence (EI). Within this context, managers and employees alike can find common ground for dealing with conflict. We need to understand and embrace how emotions fit into the workplace.

In chapter 6, additional advice is provided on how to meet the challenge of conflict head on. Avoidance of conflict, as was illustrated in the workplace violence chapter earlier, can be a prescription for disaster. Chapter 7 continues with the theme of analyzing institutional cultures for better understanding of your particular work setting.

We conclude this section with the concept of leadership. Once the tools of conflict management are understood and can be utilized, library managers are free to develop leadership capabilities, which are essential for rising to our greatest abilities. Every day, library staff and librarians show great leadership potential; recognizing and rewarding this potential in people are critical to our future success.

5

⌣•◦▲◦•⌣

A Place to Begin:
Emotional Intelligence

THIS CHAPTER SHARES SOME IDEAS AND PRACTICES THAT WE, AS SUPERVISORS, have found to be of value, but its objective is to answer these questions:

> What is emotional intelligence (EI)? How does it differ from our widely known measure of cognitive intelligence commonly known as the intelligence quotient (IQ)?
>
> Where does this concept come from, and on what theories and research is it based?
>
> Most importantly, why should it matter to us, and how can we use EI in our work environment and management style?
>
> Can and how do library managers, if we see the value of EI, bring it into the workplace?

More commonly than in years past, librarians are coming to librarianship from business management backgrounds. Several librarians who answered our survey mentioned how similar yet different the world of personnel management is in private industry compared to nonprofit or academic environments. One of the most puzzling aspects these librarians perceived as the difference between working in academia as opposed to the private sector was the lack of attention paid to and value placed on supervisory skills. The ability to work successfully with staff and colleagues did not seem to be valued, despite the fact that we manage people and budgets, give service, and furnish a product to a variety of constituents.[1]

For many in librarianship, there is a resistance to the very idea that the management of personnel and workplace practices is something to be paid any serious attention. However, survey respondents also stated that things are changing. Professional librarians are, for the most part, aware of the vital role they play in the lives of their staff and see how those relationships impact the effectiveness and overall health of their institutions. Many institutions, in partial recognition of the importance of these skills to elements like job performance, will attempt to employ a "quick fix" to the knowledge gap by occasionally resorting to what is known as the "spray and pray approach" (Caudron 1999). This is the classic scenario of a trainer appearing for a one-day seminar on a topic such as "Getting Along with Each Other." The trainer does his or her "show," pockets a check, and is gone in eight hours. "They spray employees with a concept, and pray that it will make a difference." This sad but all-too-common tale of wasted time, effort, and money comes from a profound lack of understanding or unwillingness to address and provide proper training regarding human behavioral issues in the workplace. Even the educational process and training issues surrounding EI are different. Author Jennifer Laabs states that teaching people to be emotionally intelligent is different from other workplace training because "developing emotional competence requires learners to unlearn old habits of thought, feeling and action that are deeply ingrained and learn new ones. Such a process takes motivation, effort, time, support and sustained practice" (Laabs 1999, 69). There is also a need for support of and commitment to the principles and success of any EI training program by management at every level of the organization. This is not a role that everyone will immediately embrace, and in fact, some may resist the idea that EI has any place in the workplace. As one librarian emphatically asked after a 1990s Charleston Conference presentation on conflict management, "What does any of this have to do with being a librarian?" No amount of dialogue could dislodge him from his conviction that the presentation had nothing to do with librarians as professionals. Perhaps some librarians will never see the value of managerial skills to our profession, but corporate America is quite aware of the concept of EI and is investing heavily in making it a developmental skill for their middle- and upper-level management. Researchers such as Hendrie Weisinger and Daniel Goleman, who have written groundbreaking books on EI and its applications to the workplace, command large speaker's fees that private industry seems only too willing to pay to improve the climate and temperament of their organizational culture. Why? Because as Weisinger indicates, in an emotionally intelligent organization, staff members are committed to and responsible for their own emotional development and management of their communication and interpersonal interactions and, in doing so, "take responsibility for using their emotional intelligence to apply these improvements to the organization as a whole" (Weisinger 1998, 212). Finally, unlike cognitive intelligence, which is genetically determined, EI is a set of skills that can be acquired and developed at any stage of life.

So what is EI? Let's start by discussing some common misperceptions about what may constitute EI.

> It is not just about expressing your feelings, telling it like it is, or "letting it all hang out." It concerns the internal management of feelings and reactions so that they are expressed appropriately and as you intended, especially when you are stressed or angry.

> EI is not about being pleasant, charismatic, or simply easy to get along with. "Sometimes . . . it means being able to confront someone with an uncomfortable truth he or she has been avoiding" (Caudron 1999). EI can also provide for the appropriate expression and acceptance of constructive criticism in an established environment of mutual trust between all parties.

> EI does not entail manipulating or suppressing your emotions or those of others. It is about the management of your impulses and your subsequent reactions so that they work for you in an appropriate and beneficial manner. This means learning to monitor your thought processes, then recognizing and identifying what is going on in your own psyche before you present yourself to the outer world. This can, in an emotionally intelligent person, take place in a matter of seconds. In an organization, it can establish a working environment where emotions can be expressed in a healthy and constructive manner and hence avoid the destructive effect of what is termed *emotional dissonance*, where "expressed emotions are in conformity with organizational norms, but clash with true feelings" (Abraham 1999, 18). These suppressed emotions, officially condoned or not, provide for an organization that appears normal yet is seething with discord, resists authority and any organizational change, and above all, demonstrates a nonproductive attitude toward the work and mission of the organization. The emotionally intelligent organization fosters the sense of trust, the sense of personal control, and the self-esteem needed for highly motivated and creative people to do their best.

EI is not about self-fulfillment or personal development. However, this learned skill has direct applications to your personal as well as your professional life.

EI is certainly not a "quick fix" for organizational dysfunction or conflict. EI is a set of behavioral skills that can be learned quickly on an individual basis but will take considerable practice at many organizational levels to transform an organization. Fortunately, EI can be implemented at any level, no matter how small the organization, department, or unit.

EI is not New Age psychobabble or a rehash of 1960s and 1970s sensitivity training. Rather, it is the latest development of the social intelligence movement, begun in the 1930s, which its founder, E. L. Thorndike, defined as "the ability to understand and manage men and women, boys and girls to act wisely in human relations" (Brust 2001, 4). EI is also related to the concept of *multiple intelligences* conceived by Howard Gardner (Salovey and Mayer 1993, 433). Most recently studied by Goleman, Jack Mayer, and Peter Salovey, EI is backed by many years of research by such institutions as Yale, Columbia, and Harvard universities.

An excellent definition of EI is found in an article by Robert Cooper and Ayman Sawaf:

> Emotional Intelligence is the ability to sense, understand and effectively apply the power and acumen of emotions as a source of human energy, information and influence. Emotional Intelligence emerges not from the musings of rarefied intellect, but from the workings of the human heart. EQ [another variation on EI is EQ, similar to IQ] isn't about sales tricks or how to work a room. And it's not about putting a good face on things, or the psychology of control, exploitation, or manipulation. The word *emotion* may be simply defined as applying "movement," either metaphorically or literally, to core feelings. It is Emotional Intelligence that motivates us to pursue our unique potential and purpose, it activates our innermost values and aspirations, transforming them from things we think about to what we live. (2001, 1)

Goleman states that "all emotions are, in essence, impulses to act, the instant plans for handling life that evolution has installed in us" (1995, 6).

The implications of these two definitions of EI to the modern workplace are immediate and profound. In recognition of the constant and often radical nature of change in the workplace, Quy Nguyen Huy asserts that there is a definite correlation between the EI of the individual and that individual's ability to adapt and thrive in a changing organizational environment. The individual's EI is carried over into the organization; hence, "the more emotionally capable an organization, the more successful will be its change efforts" (1999, 333). As Shari Caudron observes, "The soft skills have become hard skills" (1999).

So why is this concept considered radical? To answer this question, we need only look at recent cultural history. In Western culture, emotions have been viewed, especially in the workplace, in a pejorative manner, favoring intellect as the measure of a person's value and success. We have created an aura or mystique around the famous IQ test. Many people can remember being told at an early age that since their IQ was at a certain level, they should never have any problems making good grades in school (or perhaps just the opposite!). We have been led to think of intelligence in terms of measurable, demonstrable skills. These skills are most often measured by the IQ test in such areas as math, music, engineering, and science. These skills are equated with success in education, work, and life in general. In actuality, research has shown that the skills measured by IQ tests "at best leave 75% of job success unexplained, and at worst 96%—in other words, it does not determine who succeeds and who fails" (O'Keefe 1998). In fact, our emotions may be essential to the correct applications of critical thought and sound decision making as they provide a balance and "a crucial dimension to raw cognitive skills" (1998).

Western culture has also historically treated emotional behaviors as if they existed at one end of the human behavioral spectrum and intellectual behaviors at the diametric opposite. Emotions have been seen as the purview of an unstable, primitive savage in desperate need of continual restraint in order to prevent chaos and anarchy. As the Industrial Revolution came into being in the mid-nineteenth century, with it came an emphasis on large organizational structures; this logical, rational managerial posture became the paradigm for future organizational cultures. Max Weber, who articulated the principles of "rational-legal bureaucracy," stated that as a "bureaucracy progresses [as a social institution] the more it is 'dehumanized,' the more completely it succeeds in eliminating from official business love, hatred, and all purely personal, irrational and emotional elements which escape calculation" (Ashforth and Humphrey 1995, 101). Emotions in the workplace have been the target of "a campaign throughout the twentieth century to control workplace emotion, principally anger" (101). That which could not be measured or quantified had no value and in fact was seen as potentially subversive to the culture of business. Small wonder that as modern Western society absorbed this paradigm shift, professions that had no emotional component arose to a position of prominence, whereas professions with a social or emotional component sank to a lower status. Hence, captains of industry and scientists became cultural heroes, while teachers, social workers, librarians, and—in some cases—clergy suffered in status and income. The gender-related economic implications of this phenomenon are obvious.

The ideal intelligent person has been portrayed as serene, detached, and emotionally aloof, whereas the person given to emotions has been characterized as volatile, sensuous, earthy, and—above all—not very intelligent. Certain racial prejudices and stereotypes were supposedly confirmed based on the idea that some groups were more emotional than the dominant culture and therefore less capable than their nonemotional counterparts. This stereotyping of the emotional person as weak and the so-called rational person as superior was glorified in literature in the character of Sherlock Holmes. In recent times, the scientist is often presented as the ideal modern person—rational, analytical, and the source of information needed to succeed or triumph over adversity. How many times has a scientist in the movies been presented as emotional unless he or she was unstable? Intellect is strong and emotion is weak!

Men in many cultures have been trained principally to be analytical and unemotional through a variety of historical traditions. Sometimes cultural rituals seem like bizarre forms of hazing. Men have been taught to look at their mothers, sisters, and wives as beings generally ruled by their emotions and therefore in need of the male's serene control and guidance. This gender assignment of emotional servitude has led to the idea that somehow, because of their supposed tendency to be emotional, women were to be, quite understandably, excluded from leadership roles in society and business. Such ideas, however unfounded in historical or present-day reality, persist to this day in spite of any demonstrations or examples to the contrary. This illusion has been in some cases considered culturally sacred and politicized in the maelstrom of the modern court of common cultural opinion. Popular assumptions were, and still are in many cases, that emotions have no role in the modern workplace. The ideal supervisor is not given to any display of emotion and is not involved in employees' lives, except when it concerns work.

KEEPING EMOTIONS IN CHECK

How was and is emotion controlled in the workplace of yesterday and today? In their article "Emotion in the Workplace: A Reappraisal," Blair E. Ashforth and Ronald H. Humphrey identify four basic methods of regulating emotions that have become institutionalized and are common practice today.

1. *Neutralizing.* Through structuring the roles, relationships, obligations, and even the language used in the workplace, emotions are neutralized. "Organizations provide a substitute for interpersonal relations" (1995, 104). Ashforth and Humphrey provide the example of hospital patients whose fears and doubts are seen as a hindrance to efficient operations. Hence, doctors and nurses present a "united front" in support of recommended procedures. Consent forms are dispatched quickly, and bedside visits are kept brief and hurried, with patients being encouraged to view their emotions as just natural nervousness (1995, 105).

2. *Buffering.* This is done when emotional contact is unavoidable, so emotionality is compartmentalized. For example, if you have a consumer problem, you call a service department or online representative, often never penetrating the technical core of the operation. "Doctors provide care for patients while receptionists collect the fees. Individuals dressed as Santa Claus or the Easter Bunny act warmly toward children while photographers sell pictures. . . . Buffering preserves the image of personal concern, untainted by commercial motives" (1995, 105).

3. *Prescribing.* This involves the regulation of the length, range, and duration of the emotional contact and expression, ensuring that "seemingly irrational impulses at least appear to conform to rational task requirements" (1995, 106). Salespeople and others in service professions are trained in how to interact with customers. They work hard to appear confident and impersonally cordial in their communications. By suppressing their true feelings, they can, like an actor, interact in a prescribed manner that gives the customer a sense of well-being. All of us unconsciously learn how to respond appropriately to these situations. When a salesclerk wishes you a "nice day," you don't question the sincerity of this signal that the social interaction is over, but you automatically respond with a cheery "You too!"

An interesting study done in the 1960s indicates that hospital "patients were taught to 'be good' by nurses who would reprimand and then avoid patients who created emotional scenes" (1995, 107).

4. *Normalizing.* This takes place "by the more or less reflexive use of normalizing and face-saving rituals" (1995, 108). Normalizing can be done by diffusing unacceptable emotions through humor, stigmatization, quick apologies, or by "reframing the meaning of the emotions" in nonemotive terms (1995, 108). For example, a person may "blow off steam" and then quickly apologize or make a joke. A person who repeatedly violates the social script or code without normalizing risks being classified as explosive or a bully. One survey respondent relayed the story of a woman who lost a set of twins and couldn't seem to "snap out" of her grieving in an appropriate time frame.[2] As supervisors, we are encouraged to normalize and redirect emotionally charged situations with comments like "Let's just stick to the facts" or "Let's not bring personalities into this!"

Rather than condemning the above-mentioned practices, we should remember just how pervasive the social regulation of emotional expression is in our modern culture. We need to develop an awareness of these restrictions to be able to exercise control over our roles within them. Combining the terms *intellect* and *emotion* was unheard of in the past. Today, however, EI is a viable theory to consider. "Emotions prioritize thinking by directing us to important information" (EQ Institute). This theory is a new concept of intelligence. It is a way of integrating your emotional and intellectual life into a workable dynamic that can be more critical to your success as a librarian and manager than even your education or technical knowledge. How many times, in your personal and professional life, have you known someone who appears intelligent yet never transforms him- or herself into a successful person? How many times have you heard someone say that a person is really intelligent but a difficult person when it comes to working with others?

One survey respondent told of attending a party for a man who was retiring after a supposed long and distinguished career as a leader at that institution. This man, well known in his field, had published and spoken at meetings. In circulating through the attendees of this reception, she soon realized that although the room was full, no one really wanted to be there. As it turned out, this distinguished scholar was almost uniformly despised by students, staff, and colleagues. It seems he was an intimidating, arrogant individual who was repeatedly characterized with the acronym "SOB." He would not be missed at the institution where he had labored for so many years. She told us that it was hard to listen to the polite accolades offered that afternoon.[3]

Studies have repeatedly shown that how your career develops over your working life could depend on your degree of EI. There is a saying becoming popular in the corporate world: "IQ gets you hired, but EQ gets you promoted" (Gibbs 1995). In a study of executives who "derailed" or failed to live up to their potential, it was found that many times these failures were caused by "interpersonal flaws rather than a technical inability" (1995). One of the most reassuring aspects of EI is that it can be learned at any point in life. With personal commitment and practice, it can be developed into a managerial and personal skill.

What are the basic skills of EI? Emotional intelligence, as defined by author and noted expert Goleman, consists of four skills: self-awareness, self-management, motivation, and empathy.

SELF-AWARENESS

"Recognizing a feeling as it happens is the keystone of Emotional Intelligence" (Goleman 1995, 43). To develop self-awareness, you learn to listen to and monitor your own thoughts and emotions. This allows you, maybe for the first time, to recognize the what and why of your own actions. You can then take charge of yourself and better control the way you respond.

An anecdote from the survey illustrates this point beautifully. The respondent observes:

> I have a dear friend who at one point in my career was my supervisor. She is a bright, talented person who should have been a director by this point in her life. If she has a flaw, it is that she has no concept of how she presents herself to others. Until you know and understand her, she appears domineering, aloof, and explosive. I've known her now for almost 20 years and have repeatedly watched her try to manage staff and colleagues. During one recent conversation, she indicated that all but three of her 29 staff members had filed a grievance against her. Her reaction was typical of her lack of her emotional awareness when she announced

"and I won in all but two of the cases." I then asked her how long each case took to resolve. She indicated between three to six weeks. My mathematical abilities told me that she was spending most of her time fighting and clearing her name. The last message I received this summer was a request for a reference, as she has agreed to step down at the end of the year.[4]

We couldn't read this story without reflecting on a quotation from Weisinger in *Emotional Intelligence at Work:* "The subjective knowledge about the nature of your personality not only guides your behavior from situation to situation . . . it also provides you with a solid framework for making better choices. . . . Lacking self-awareness, you lack sufficient information to make effective decisions" (1998, 4–6).

One of the first steps in gaining self-awareness is learning to monitor your own internal dialogue and your inner thought processes. Have you ever listened to your own critical self-evaluations? Known as "negative self-talk," these are the little voices in your head that say things such as "I'm going to make a mess of this" or "I don't know how to deal with this!" On the other hand, you can focus on positive affirmations such as "I am going to be fine during this meeting; I know what I'm doing." These negative and positive self-evaluations, if not recognized and managed, may become self-fulfilling prophecies for better or worse.

A second step toward monitoring this internal dialogue is, according to Weisinger, using the phrase "I think" in your statements. Weisinger points out that "by intentionally utilizing 'I think' statements, you clarify what you think and you also recognize that you are the person responsible for your appraisals" (1998, 7). By essentially talking with ourselves and monitoring our own inner dialogue, most of us will begin to recognize patterns or "scripts" (ways of responding to certain stressors and situations) that play like a recording through our thought processes. These behavioral scripts were most likely not written by ourselves but are often generated by and similar to those scripts found in our primary family structure. Without knowing it, we bring these scripts with us to work.

We bring an entire set of behaviors, both positive and negative, that subtly if not unconsciously influence how we will cope with relationships, stressful situations, and, especially, conflict. If your family dealt with stress by explosive or threatening dialogue, emotional outbursts, or passive-aggressive put-downs, there is a high degree of probability that you will respond to stressful situations at work in the same manner, possibly to your great detriment. If your family members withdrew and were uncommunicative when angry, you are probably going to have a difficult time expressing yourself in an assertive manner when confronted. Monitoring your inner dialogue allows you to ask yourself, "Is this what I really think? Do I really have all the facts here?"

It is critical to realize that the evaluation, not the action, is what is directing your reaction—and the evaluation is yours. Make certain it is actually working for you, not against you. If you have had an encounter that has not gone well or has left you confused, wait until you have calmed down and then analyze what took place, both externally and, most importantly, internally. It is also valuable to realize that your evaluations of people and events are and should be subject to change. For example, maybe you did not actually know why those people at the meeting were whispering, and maybe it was not about you at all. It is very important to make certain you heard what a person actually thought he or she said. Monitoring your own internal dialogue at these times can often reveal an unconscious bias and allow you to properly interpret what you see and how you react.

A third step toward self-awareness is to be aware of how your *physical reactions* to stressful situations manifest in yourself. Your physical senses provide data for your evaluation of and subsequent reactions to situations and people. For example, you are presenting in a meeting, and a colleague seems to be scowling at you during your presentation. Your neck begins to tighten, your stomach clenches, or your palms sweat as the fear sets in and you begin to internally respond. Without thinking, you ask yourself, What does this mean? You may quickly determine that he looks angry or that he is upset with you for some reason. The physical response starts an emotionally generated chain reaction and a possible script of fear-based emotional dialogue. A more accurate interpretation would be to acknowledge that you see a frown, or you see him looking at the ceiling, and nothing more. Your physical reaction to what you thought you saw can immediately trigger an emotionally charged sequence that could undermine your presentation or initiate an inappropriate reaction like a confrontation.

It is critical to be able to recognize in yourself your own individual physical reactions to stress. By identifying their presence, you may be able to disrupt the chain before you react. As we have seen, your first reaction to the colleague may be correct or it may be a misinterpretation. The second is an acknowledgment of what you are experiencing and gives you time for an additional, possibly more accurate interpretation. Suppose later the same day you approach that colleague who was frowning during your presentation, and he admits that he was thinking about a fight he had that morning with his spouse. You were correct in noting his facial expression, but its cause had nothing to do with your presentation. You also need, as Weisinger contends, to look at the manner in which you present yourself publicly. Do you automatically cross your arms when you are nervous? Do you make eye contact with your staff or do you allow your eyes to wander the room? The way you present yourself will give a signal to the other person(s) involved, for better or worse (1998, 15–16).

To practice these concepts, next time you are in a big meeting, pay attention to people. What are they doing? How are they speaking to each other? What sort of physical signals are they giving each other? Sit back and just observe. You will begin to realize how all these sensory data subtly affect your evaluations and subsequent reactions. One place to begin to consciously observe yourself and your physical and emotional reactions is in the observation of your own family members during a social event.

This form of self-awareness does not come easily to most of us. It can bring up painful memories as we become aware of the feelings we have and how and where they developed into our reactions. Most of us try to avoid what is painful. We deny, we rationalize, we divert—none of which will serve us well. Trying to push your feelings into an emotional box is like trying to contain water under pressure in a paper envelope. As soon as we think we have contained it, a leak appears somewhere. The most important fact to realize is that your evaluations and reactions are your own. People will invariably behave toward you in inexplicable manners. You may not be able to control that, but you can control how you react internally and externally by developing a heightened awareness of your own inner processes.

You can also begin to discover what your own intentions are in work situations. Your intentions refer to those "immediate desires, what you would like to accomplish today" (Weisinger 1998, 19). As Weisinger indicates, your own intentions may not be easy to discern; you may have unconscious agendas that have nothing to do with work (1998, 19). For instance, you might struggle with feelings of inadequacy caused by an external condition or early experience in your life. Perhaps a parent or your spouse has ridiculed your choice of profession. ("Librarians are wimps"; "Librarians are shy and retiring spinsters"; "Librarians aren't really faculty [professionals, etc.]"; and so forth.) You may "act out" at work in ways that help you compensate for the underlying need to prove yourself. You might, for example, exercise obsessively to not look "wimpy," or you might dress in a certain manner so as to appear more sophisticated. Admitting to conflicting inner motivations takes being honest with yourself and developing a sense of trust with what you are feeling.

With heightened self-awareness, we can start to monitor and manage our actions and reactions and see end results of all the other motivations and feelings that are visible to others. For a description of the many exercises and techniques you can use for working on your own self-awareness, we recommend that you review Weisinger's *Emotional Intelligence at Work*, where he also outlines in detail techniques of self-management.

SELF-MANAGEMENT

Managing your emotions means understanding them and then using that understanding to turn situations to your benefit. To accomplish this form of management, you will need to have control of at least three components of your emotional system (Weisinger 1998, 27):

- Your thoughts or cognitive appraisals
- Your physiological changes or arousal actions
- Your behaviors or action tendencies

Learning to manage these components allows you to take control of yourself in a way many of us never do. For example, you may have issues that really "push your buttons." Monitoring your inner dialogue can reveal negative or counterproductive scripts that just seem to appear out of nowhere. Some psychologists call these "automatic thoughts," and they may appear as the first reaction in an uncensored or spontaneous manner. You might react with such thoughts as "You never listen to me," "You selfish bastard," or "You never treat me with respect." These types of thoughts trigger almost immediate acceptance on our part and trigger other auto-scripts, for example, "There she goes again, trying to assert her dominance by finding fault with everything I do" or "I wish she would get fired, that incompetent idiot." These dialogues can keep repeating themselves and are hard to shut down without practice. Worst of all, they can lead to distorted evaluations and reactions.

Anger is probably one of the most difficult emotions to manage. Often based in a fear reaction, anger physiologically comes from the older, more primitive part of the brain. The human brain, through millions of years of development, can generate anger or fear that is incredibly powerful and intense. This is the type of reaction that caused our ancestors to flee or fight their predators. It's a survival reaction honed over thousands of generations. Since we are no longer fending off wild animals, a strong "fight-or-flight" reaction can cause distorted thinking and reactions. Goleman describes this ancient reaction as centering in the brain area called the amygdala. Designed as a neurological survival mechanism, the amygdala is physically designed to react instantly to fear stimulus from the thalamus and alert the body to take immediate action. It remembers threatening stimuli and provides an instant response before the brain has time to literally think it out. As Goleman states, "The amygdala can house memories and response repertoires that we enact without quite realizing why we do so because the shortcut from the thalamus to the amygdala completely bypasses the neocortex" (1995, 18). This old evolutionary reaction does not give us time to reason out whether we are really in danger. Although this is fine for escaping a tiger, such a reaction in the modern workplace often leads us to respond in ways we never intended. One survey respondent told of an employee who had seen combat in Vietnam and would often react to loud noises by leaping under his desk only to emerge sheepishly as soon as his reasoning brain caught up with his amygdala.[5] Other less extreme responses might include making sudden verbal outbursts or throwing objects. One should reflect on the advice commonly given to parents when their children are causing them stress: "Stop and think before you pick up your child." Reacting before thinking can be dangerous in unintended ways. One of the quickest ways to recognize this primal fear reaction is to learn how your body reacts when frightened or otherwise stressed. When you are upset (either because of fear or anger), you typically breathe faster, your heartbeat quickens, and adrenaline is released, putting you in a heightened state of awareness. Some people start shutting off other, nonessential senses like hearing and smell when they are angry or frightened and liken the experience to being in a tunnel or a dream. Researchers have found that you can disrupt these physical reactions and not allow them to overwhelm you so that you can think clearly. One simple method is to breathe deeply several times and visualize something that you have always associated with serenity. It may be a special place you are fond of, such as a lake, beach, or some other peaceful setting. If this technique, referred to as "the relaxation response," is practiced, it can give you the time you need to balance and center yourself along with starting a constructive inner dialogue. There is nothing wrong with interrupting a negative dialogue or situation with a trip to the restroom or a walk down the hall. The important thing is to disrupt the negative cycle.

A survey respondent told of a female coworker who came into his office screaming obscenities. He stood up, said, "Excuse me," and headed down the hall, his coworker following behind, still yelling, until he reached the safety of the men's restroom. He went into a stall, closed his eyes, began breathing deeply, and calmed himself down. We can only hope that his colleague found a quiet spot where she too could calm down.[6] This is an excellent example of managing a stressful situation without allowing it to escalate by reacting in fear to a verbal assault.

In addition to learning to use the relaxation response, you can take other steps to help cool down an angry coworker or lighten up a tense situation.

Your Internal Indicators of Stress

As you learn to manage your reactions and monitor your internal mental dialogue, watch out for these other subtle psychological indicators:

> *Avoid overgeneralizations.* Statements like "This happens every time," "I'm in big trouble," or "I always end up blamed for things" will only escalate the situation. First of all, most of these statements are probably old negative scripts that attack and lower your self-esteem. A classic, well-demonstrated method of controlling or manipulating people as individuals or as a group is to attack their sense of self-worth, characterizing each mishap as a critical failure. After a while, the criticism becomes internalized, and the controller does not have to directly apply it anymore. This is a key element of interpersonal dynamics used by religious cults. Maintaining negative self-esteem as a control strategy has been a cornerstone of such groups, often with disastrous results. You may have unconsciously absorbed such scripts in earlier years, and they can present themselves automatically in your work life—to your detriment.

> *Avoid negative labeling of yourself and others.* Learning to observe and control your mind's internal dialogue usually helps to limit this sort of behavior. The idea is not just to avoid distorted thinking but also to develop constructive dialogues. As an example, instead of a negative script, a constructive response might be, "Why does this make me so angry?" or "What's really happening here?" This is a signal to yourself to start working this out in a positive manner.

Avoid "mind reading" when interacting with others (Goleman 1995, 33). Regardless of how well you believe you know people, you are not privy to their innermost thoughts and feelings unless they express them to you. Avoid statements like "I know what you're thinking!" or "OK, now you're mad!" Remember, you may not be reading the signals correctly, and your assessment of another person's mental state will almost surely be rejected and resented, further hindering communication. No one truly knows why others are behaving the way they are, and sometimes we ourselves do not understand our own behavior. Unless you are a trained therapist and you are being paid to counsel, don't fall into this trap. It's also positive and constructive to communicate your anger in a statement of fact. "I'd like you to know that I am beginning to become angry and upset" or "I'd like to stop arguing and take a moment to calm down and think more clearly. Why don't we get together in thirty minutes to work out this issue?" Only a bully or someone eager for confrontation will want to remain engaged at this point. You are not required to stand and fight it out.

Don't make silent rules and internal contracts for how others should behave without communicating these rules to them. As Weisinger states, "By having rules for how people should act, you set yourself up for much disappointment and anger because people very often don't behave as we want" (1998, 33). As a result, we feel betrayed or wronged when no agreement to do otherwise ever existed outside your own head.

All of these methods are valuable to diffuse a tense situation. They will give you the time needed to define what has upset you, disrupt the negative dialogues, identify your intentions and reactions, perhaps change your assessment of the situation, generate alternatives to resolving the problem, and define better ways of accomplishing your objectives. Then you can approach the person and the issue once again.

One other suggestion offered is to use humor to calm down or to diffuse your own or another person's anger. This can be a risky response, though, and should only be employed in certain situations. Humor applied to already tense situations may in fact escalate negativity, since people may interpret your humor as an indication that you don't take them seriously or are dismissing their issue as a joke. One survey respondent expressed a growing resentment at his supervisor's treating his concerns as a joke, making him feel as though he were being set up for ridicule.[7] The supervisor may have been unconsciously employing an internal script utilizing humor to diffuse tension, but the employee was interpreting this reaction in a negative way.

Learn to redirect your own negative energy. Make a conscious decision to be aware that you are stressed and do something to help you cope, preferably something requiring physical activity. When upset with situations at work, one person may go home and play the piano furiously; another might mix clay for pottery projects with great gusto. It often helps to sit down and outline your issue on paper in order to visualize it and the solution more clearly. Several authors suggest keeping a journal of difficult interactions as a way of chronicling and reflecting on the events and emotions and how you responded. This practice allows you to clearly identify your emotional triggers and when and under what circumstances they occur so that you can avoid situations that provoke your automatic reactions.

MOTIVATION

Goleman states that "motivation technically is expending energy in a specific direction for a specific purpose" (1995, 6). In regard to EI, it means being able to recognize and promote your own self-worth and confidence to inspire you to start, follow through, and complete the project at hand. It means using "the power of positive thinking" to stay focused but also to adapt to the inevitable changes that present themselves on a rather constant basis in today's libraries. One useful technique is mental imagery. Imagine yourself accomplishing the task you're working on. One of the exercises in motivation that Weisinger and others suggest is to assign yourself meaningful, achievable goals that you know you can accomplish, monitor your behavior, and build your momentum to overcome the expected setbacks. Every project of any size has elements that go awry. As a supervisor, one of your chief managerial responsibilities is not only solving problems as they arise but also setting an example for staff in your department in terms of their reactions to unexpected setbacks. Like it or not, as the supervisor, you set the tone and the mood for how staff react to stress. If you respond as if every setback were a disaster, pretty soon staff will respond in kind. Developing an optimistic behavioral posture is a fundamental element in managing organizational change in any form.

Acknowledge difficulties but move on to alternative solutions to allow you and your staff to reenergize, then refocus on the problems and issues involved. Like managing emotions evoked by change in the workplace, every technique of EI may be employed during difficult times as you move through the stages of grief: from disbelief, anger, nostalgia for "the good old days," depression, acceptance, and, finally, hope. Positive energy will eventually return. That same pattern of reaction occurs when major change or significant disruption is foisted upon an organizational group.

Cultivation of supportive friends, family, and colleagues is important to give and receive the kind of emotional and motivational support you need to survive in today's workplace. This can be hard for some, especially those who were taught to keep their problems to themselves. Ideally, you look for someone who you can trust, who is suitable for the situation, and who can be available when you need to talk. The goal is to be able to face things in a more positive manner, get the balance and feedback you need, and, as a result, handle problems and stress in a way you perhaps wouldn't have thought possible. If you avail yourself of this benefit, you should also be willing to provide the same assistance to others that they provided to you. Learning to listen effectively to others and respond adequately to their emotional needs can build your organization into a positive, cohesive, and productive unit.

EMPATHY

Empathy is another critical component of EI. Individuals who lack the ability to empathize with others often end up in the news as having committed heinous criminal acts. Complete lack of empathy is one of the main personality traits of sex offenders and serial killers. Inmate therapy programs that focus on "perspective-taking" of the victim help increase empathy skills in such offenders (Goleman 1995, 106). Unfortunately, hardened psychopaths are usually beyond such efforts, and certain types of learning disabilities prevent the development of empathy in some individuals. However, for most of us it is more likely that we simply need to get beyond self-absorption and become aware of others around us. Empathy, like all the other components of EI, can be cultivated and improved upon at any age.

Empathy is considered an essential managerial component for the ability to counsel employees in a professional manner without straying into a clinical posture. Madonna G. Constantine and Kathy A. Gainor define empathy in the school setting as the "counselor's ability to communicate a sense of caring and understanding regarding their clients' experiences" (2001, 131). Furthermore, "empathy requires the accurate identification of emotional responses in others" (2001, 131). If a supervisor has empathy, he or she will be better able to recognize and correctly interpret the emotional states and reactions of others. Empathy allows a supervisor to recognize when it is the most appropriate time for a meeting, for proposing new ideas, for discussing issues regarding performance, or for interrupting or getting involved in an interpersonal conflict. As Goleman adds, "People's emotions are rarely put into words; far more often they are expressed in other cues" (1995, 96). For example, an employee who is sitting and staring vacantly into space may not tell you he or she is worried over a sick child. Empathy allows the supervisor to approach in a supportive manner that will help the person express his or her concern and then return to the task at hand. Without empathy, the supervisor observes only that this person is not working. Approaching the person in an unfeeling manner may do more harm than good. Earlier in this chapter we reviewed the importance of being able to read correctly or not misread a person's facial expressions, body posture, tone of voice, and so forth. Empathy is also an essential element of any in-service training session as the instructor must be able to gauge adequately the audience reactions to the presentation and the rate at which the material is being absorbed. In the daily work environment, empathy can be a valuable tool for interpreting and eventually interrupting a cycle of conflict. Given the ethnically and culturally diverse environment of the modern workplace, empathy allows for better and more effective communication.

MANAGING YOUR RELATIONSHIPS

The final component or, some say, the end result of EI involves effective communication, the proper amount of assertiveness to put your ideas across, and the ability to listen and empathize, to take and give constructive criticism, and to work successfully in group or team situations—in short, being able to effectively manage your personal communications and your interpersonal relationships in a productive and effective manner. As a supervisor, one needs to learn how to communicate effectively with a wide variety of personality types, cultural and social elements, and educational levels, and there is no set standard or expected outcome that will work for everyone.

Our survey produced many types of responses and comments. As each was reviewed, it became apparent that many librarians see their work environments in a very positive manner and look forward to going to work. As these surveys were reviewed, a trend in the responses began to emerge. Statements indicated that in such environments, people felt as if they could be open in their communications, felt a climate of fairness pervaded the organization, felt they had access to supervisors if problems arose, felt trusted and valued as employees and professionals, and felt they were considered responsible for their behavior in their interpersonal work relations. The overall tone of their responses suggested an enlightened work environment where the skills of EI were valued and practiced. One typical example follows: "Our library does have a supportive and friendly environment where people are told when they are doing a good job and that they are valued as employees of the library. We always know what is expected of us and when we do not come up to expectations are questioned as to any problems either at work or home that might be contributing to the problem. Ways are suggested for improvement, and you are always given a second chance to meet expectations."[8]

Such success is often measured on a person-to-person basis that evolves into a group dynamic over time. Many observers have suggested that our society needs to return to basic courtesies and manners that were considered necessary for common conduct in the past. Manners are nice and make social interactions more predictable, but they don't guarantee social success. Better might be the acceptance of theories like EI as an organizational development that evolves from within each employee rather than one that's imposed from outside.

In summation, EI is not the answer to being successful in the workplace and in life in general; however, it does have potential as a method of integrating the intellect with the emotional parts of our personalities. It involves starting with yourself as a person, professional librarian, and manager.

NOTES

1. Survey respondent 55, academic librarian, June 2, 2000; survey respondent 172, academic librarian, June 5, 2000; survey respondent 349, academic librarian, June 12, 2000.

2. Survey respondent 339, public librarian, June 16, 2000.

3. Survey respondent 144, academic librarian, June 5, 2000.
4. Survey respondent 334, special librarian, June 11, 2000.
5. Survey respondent 155, academic library support staff, June 5, 2000.
6. Survey respondent 221, special librarian, June 9, 2000.
7. Survey respondent 227, academic librarian, June 7, 2000.
8. Survey respondent 79, public librarian, June 5, 2000.

6

Planning for Workplace Conflict

EXPECTING CONFLICT ALLOWS YOU TO PREPARE AND, AT TIMES, TO MITIGATE the level of conflict or avoid it altogether. As observed in earlier chapters, changes in the work environment may cause stress and generate fear, possibly bringing forth undesirable behavior even in the best employees. These behaviors are often symptomatic of social and environmental pressures that have been building for quite some time. Especially during times of organizational change and transition, staff benefit from management's example to navigate the turbulence. The presence of conflict can offer us an opportunity to examine and identify those pressures and manage their impact. This is essential for leading staff and oneself through times of transition, which are a constant rather than an exception in today's work environment. Management's leadership and modeled vision are needed to form a strategic approach. Otherwise, excellent ideas for improvements may never reach fruition, and our best efforts at implementing change may be met with indifference, crippling resistance, and even possible sabotage of your efforts.

LEARN TO BE OBSERVANT

As we have seen in the scenarios and survey, attempting to avoid conflict often engenders it. John Provost Wilkinson and Margaret Ann Wilkinson advocate the correlation of management style to the "employee's level of 'work maturity'" (1997, 206). Paul Hersey and Kenneth Blanchard base this idea on studies in their text, *Management of Organizational Behavior* (1977, 209). Managers learn to expect various types of responses to organizational conflict based on the level at which an employee works. This requires the manager to observe each employee and take the time to recognize and understand that person's mode of analysis and reactions to various sets of circumstances. Empathetic connection between the manager and employee will satisfy emotional and social objectives while accomplishing the institution's goals as well. One way to accomplish this goal of awareness is for the manager to observe employee reactions during meetings, evaluations, or periods of stress as well as general social skills exhibited on a daily basis. For example, does an employee tend to respond to stressful situations by making a joke or finding humor in the matter? Such a process will eventually reveal that person's level of work maturity *and* demonstrate the goals, agendas, or expectations the employee may have with regard to his or her work.

Moshe Cohen asserts, "The first step in addressing any conflict is awareness. Too often situations that breed conflict go unnoticed for long periods of time until the issues are truly intractable" (1998, 19). How many of us, as supervisors, have learned about an interpersonal conflict in our department only after it erupted as a verbal disagreement involving everyone nearby? It is all too easy to become engrossed in our daily assignments and remain physically and psychologically in our office for most of the day. In certain types of library settings, supervisors do not receive any acknowledgment or kudos for their ability to manage people effectively. This skill may not be taken into consideration when tenure or promotion decisions are made. This indifference possibly has its roots in the lack of attention paid to managerial skills in library master's programs, where management is sometimes treated as an afterthought. As one survey respondent quipped, referring to staff conflicts, "I didn't become a librarian to deal with this stuff!"[1]

Any level of effective supervision requires alertness to the psychological and emotional ambience of a work area and the people therein, with a constant monitoring of the social climate. It is in every manager's direct self-interest to know the scuttlebutt and to be able to spot the symptoms of an emerging conflict. A proactive strategy of monitoring can be as simple as greeting people each morning and taking note of their responses. For example, if a normally good-natured employee seems preoccupied or overly stressed, or doesn't seem to be working as usual, it might be a good idea to wait a while and then wander out onto the floor, stopping at the employee's desk. When you engage the person, if he or she seems to still be out of character, it is well within your purview to say something like, "You don't seem quite yourself today. Is everything OK? Is there anything I can help you with?" Usually, if you have taken the time to establish and maintain an open communication stance, the person will confide in you. Such an employee may deny any problem at that moment, only to appear in your office later that day to discuss the issue. The role of watchful counselor is one too often neglected in the workplace for fear of being thought of as intrusive or being a busybody. Each day you work as a supervisor, you establish and reestablish the kind of social culture that directly affects your workplace. Many issues and conflicts, if caught in the early stages, can be easily resolved or mediated before they smolder and then finally erupt later.

Taking a reactive stance or waiting till conflict erupts usually means you will spend a great deal of time trying to distinguish the manifestations of conflict from the actual issues that engendered it in the first place. In planning for conflict, we can look to the same principles involved in addressing personnel issues during periods of organizational change.

WATCH FOR DIFFERENT PERCEPTIONS OF WORK

When people come into conflict with each other, it often is because of "goal incompatibility" (Wilkinson and Wilkinson 1997, 209). If, for example, an employee views herself as the logical choice for a certain promotion, she may not be as receptive to changes in the organizational structure if this change does not result in the desired promotion. (See "Scenario 1: The Internal Candidate.") An individual's level of expectation combined with perceived goals translates into levels of motivation and perception relative to the work. The Wilkinsons also point to how people perceive their access to and ability to use and allocate job-related resources. Their perceptions will affect the way in which they interact with others and produce on a daily basis (1997, 206). For example, if a Technical Services librarian, because of unique job demands, is not able to attend conferences or conduct the level of research commonly expected by peers in public service positions, the librarian may have feelings of alienation and isolation that, in turn, may translate into interdepartmental conflict.

MANAGERIAL STYLE

Your own accessibility is critical to the success of your information gathering and effective communication. Do employees view you as someone who is easily approached? Does your management style facilitate or hinder the flow of communication between you, staff, and colleagues? What kind of culture does your department have? What is the overall culture of your institution? What do your colleagues, staff, and others say about the culture of your organization? Whether or not you agree with their assessment, their perceptions will, to a large degree, determine how they will act and interact within the workplace. One of the reasons we sought anecdotal rather than statistical data through our survey was to solicit the perceptions that determine the responses, regardless of what the statistics indicate.

As we saw in the chapter on the development of emotional intelligence as a managerial skill, this type of careful, critical analysis can be indispensable when working with the organizational culture, no matter how small your portion of it may be. In *The Character of a Corporation*, Rob Goffee and Gareth Jones define culture as "a common way of thinking which drives a common way of acting on the job or producing a product" (1998, 15). The overall strength of an internal organizational culture "is about sustainability" (1998, 15). The success of a library's efforts to innovate, grow, and remain a vital asset to its parent institution eventually depends upon "the nature of the relationships within the organization—the way people act toward each other, the 'social capital' of the organization" (1998, 15). Whether out of ignorance, fear, or indolence, librarians have too long sought solace from the task of managing conflict and instead have focused energy on the promotion of technological innovations, often while their organizational core decayed. As a result, innovations may be overshadowed by inner conflicts. No manager can legitimately claim to lead a department or library of any size without knowledge of the internal organizational culture of the institution. As we repeatedly observed from the survey, employees know the difference between legitimate, involved leadership and an absent or symbolic form of leadership. As one survey respondent reported, "Our director is a fraud as far as leadership. He does nothing but hide from the personnel problems that plague this library. We will all be glad when he retires."[2]

Effective management is an ongoing process. Dealing with these issues is certainly costly and time-consuming. In their article on the economics of conflict, Randall Poe and Carol Lee Courter state that, in the corporate sector, "staff conflicts cost corporate managers more than nine weeks of working time each year" (1996, 5). A large part of the problem is that most administrators take a reactive rather than proactive stance, waiting for fully developed conflicts to manifest. This simply is not a psychologically healthy, managerially competent, or economically acceptable position for anyone in a supervisory role to take.

CHANGE: A MAJOR SOURCE OF CONFLICT

It has long been recognized that organizational change itself can be a major catalyst for organizational conflict. William Bridges, in *Managing Transitions*, describes the internal human response to external change as *transition*. He asserts, "Transition is the psychological process people go through to come to terms with the new situation. Change is external, transition is internal." He goes on to say, "Unless transition occurs, change will not work" (1991, 3).

Regarding the difference between change and transition, Bridges notes that "when we talk about change, we naturally focus on the outcome that the change will produce" (1991, 4). In cases of interpersonal conflict, we often focus too quickly on bringing the argumentative aspects to a halt, mistaking the outward manifestation for the actual cause. Bridges observes, "Transition is different. The starting point for transition is not the outcome, but the ending that you have to make to leave the old situation behind" (4). In conflict management, we want to bring people safely through the manifestation phase of conflict, allowing them to voice their concerns fully, look for points of reconciliation, and move them, if possible, to some point of resolution.

Our institutions' attitudes and policies toward change events in our work lives are also a prime cause of what is termed *emotional dissonance*. As Rebecca Abraham states, "Emotional dissonance occurs when expressed emotions are in conformity with organizational norms, but clash with true feelings" (1999, 18). Many libraries and other institutions have approached change events with a "We're going to put a brave face on all of this and move forward" posture, which often requires individuals to stoically repress any anxiety or other feelings they may have toward the move. One survey respondent told of being required to present a failed institutional program as a success and, upon pain of termination, tell no one how much money had been wasted.[3] This respondent spoke of the emotional drain and negative psychological toll that was endured by the staff during and after this period.

Unfortunately, most of us at some point in our careers are going to have to participate in and support policies, programs, or people in whom we do not have faith. We will, therefore, experience some degree of emotional dissonance. Abraham examines the impact of being made to pretend that something is true when it is not and states that one way to counter the discomfort is to try to give people a sense of self-esteem and self-confidence in the face of the dissonance. "Workers given a high degree of autonomy are able to cope effectively with emotional dissonance" (1999, 23). Allowing for personal autonomy and promoting self-esteem and a sense of competence in those exposed to the stress of change events represent a conscious effort on the part of management to promote a positive work environment. Such a posture must be genuine and should function at all levels of the organization.

THE DUAL NATURE OF THE WORKPLACE CULTURE

Most of us are aware of at least two major dimensions of social reality in the workplace. First, there is the public dimension, characterized by our formal culture of mission statements, policies, procedures, and certain behaviors associated with the public persona the organization presents to the outside world. There is also a private dimension of our work environment that, though often not openly acknowledged, may in fact be the major dynamic element within an organization. This dimension contains all the subtle communications, unspoken and unwritten rules for conduct, and unacknowledged modes of interaction. This inner world of work is often where most of the organizational stress and conflict will occur and where, because of its unofficial and often unrecognized position, conflict is the most difficult to address. As in a dysfunctional family, a poisonous environment may lurk beneath what appears to be a solid, thriving organization. In at least a half dozen of the surveys, an administrator or department head presented a positive face to a particular organization. However, responses from other librarians and staff from the same institution told a very different story—one of social strife and profound dissonance. In short, the organization looked healthy outwardly but was, in fact, "a toxic organization" (Coccia 1998, 32). Cynthia Coccia defines such an organization as "one that thrives on control and exists in a constant state of crisis, and depends on disasters and impending doom to make changes. Such change is often a short-term fix, rather than a well-thought-out solution to a problem. This kind of organization stifles creativity, controls information and impedes decision making" (1998, 33). Coccia indicates that little can be done at lower levels to repair such organizations, and it is best to avoid them.

Three survey respondents told of giving up well-paying positions for lesser positions after struggling for years in toxic organizations.[4] What can be done to heal such an organization? Generally, this level of organizational dysfunction will require intervention from the outside and will result in major career changes for many of those still involved. Although this book generally adopts a position of self-empowerment and supports positive solutions to the issues of conflict, it is also essential to be able to recognize when a work situation is too dysfunctional and exceeds your ability to adapt or influence it. To abandon an unhealthy situation is actually a sign of personal wisdom and savvy career management.

CHARACTERISTICS OF SOCIAL STRESS DURING PERIODS OF CHANGE

The stresses of change and transition in the modern library workplace are certainly not uncommon. When you started at a new school, took your first professional position in a library, got married or committed to a new partner, had children, got divorced, or moved to a new residence, some part of your life changed forever; generally, you found yourself having to let go of some element of your previous life. The loss of old friends, of the sense of personal well-being and familiarity, of feelings of competence, and of other such elements of your life may be a difficult adjustment. We have all gone through such experiences of transition. Bridges outlines the specific stages as follows:

> A *loss of a sense of personal identity*. Conflict, like change, places people emotionally in a state of limbo that requires them to examine themselves and their relationships in light of their new situation. This can lead to disorientation.
>
> *Feelings of disorientation*. Bridges defines this neutral zone as an "emotional wilderness" (1991, 5). The travel industry refers to something similar as "culture shock." Conflict in the workplace, especially where a violent verbal or physical encounter results, can leave even noninvolved people with symptoms of post-traumatic stress that may linger for years. One respondent to our survey told of panic attacks, disturbed sleep, and eventually her own job abandonment following an act of violence that occurred in her library, a result of an interpersonal conflict. "I found myself unable to focus, crying in the restroom, and being filled with fear every time I went to work. I ended up leaving a well-paying job for a lesser position in another city."[5]
>
> *Heightened anxiety and self-doubt*. Feelings of resentment and defensiveness emerge. Many of us have found in our professional lives that a new job is the quickest way to find out what you did

not know or did not learn from previous positions. Conflict resulting from change events in the workplace often reintroduces
unrelated psychological wounds long pushed into the recesses
of our minds. One survey respondent relayed that her current
supervisor's angry outbursts brought back vivid memories of
verbal and physical abuse from childhood. "I find myself with-
drawing into my own little world, where no one can hurt me.
Sometimes, I can't even hear his words anymore."[6] Certainly,
the supervisor is probably not aware of the effect his outburst is
producing and may be finding the employee's silent withdrawal
and lack of engagement frustrating if not puzzling.

Grief. Grief often emerges with a longing for times past, even if
those times were troubled, and a "halo effect" may form. As
you attempt to manage and resolve conflict within an organization where conflict has been the norm, you will often find a
strange nostalgia for the period before there was an attempt to
reconcile.

Denial. As Catherine Petrini and Kenneth Hultman indicate, "Leaders
maintain that these changes are necessary to survive, but a lot
of employees simply don't believe it. They believe the changes
are just another way to get more work out of them" (1995, 16).

As we have seen earlier, several bits of information to surface from the
survey indicated the need for administrators to address openly the conflict
within their organizations. Denial or avoidance of organizational conflict on
the part of supervisors and administrators has almost universally been interpreted by staff as an indifference to the organizational culture and as a clear
indicator of professional ineptitude. On the other hand, a proactive and involved posture has been repeatedly demonstrated to be a key factor in the
amount of satisfaction and loyalty employees felt toward their jobs and
those who supervise them. Such symptoms may translate into conflict that
you may not recognize immediately. There are several ways to analyze and
subsequently approach your organizational conflict.

Bridges recommends that when we face a growing conflict situation, we
should analyze each event and position in a department or organization
(1991). As supervisors, we need to identify and understand what actual issues are involved, including those that may not readily present themselves,
such as hidden agendas and unforeseen factors resulting from the conflict.
We also need to be able to identify whether the issues are actually work

related or have their origin in some other situation like conflicts of a personal nature. Often, careful, unbiased listening during the dialogue will reveal what is actually happening. In some cases, the principals in the conflict may not be fully aware of what is causing their problem.

The following are examples of displaced conflict. One survey respondent described a heated encounter over cataloging procedures that actually had its origins in a failed love relationship.[7] Another ongoing conflict that was related by a colleague actually had roots in a centuries-long ethnic conflict in Southeast Asia but on the surface appeared to be a problem concerning work-flow issues and productivity. Disclosing your perceptions of alternate or hidden issues must be handled in a careful, diplomatic manner to avoid becoming entangled in the conflict yourself. Asking the following questions can help supervisors to focus on the conflict at hand and its roots.

> Who is actually involved? This is the time to look for a possible third party or even a "helpful antagonist." Many times, as consultant Pat Wagner has indicated, there is an outside third party who is acting as a conduit for communication between two parties but has no real role in the conflict. Often, interpersonal conflict results from this "triangulation," or broken and intercepted communication (1999). Is this issue contained within this group or is some outside entity involved?

> What are the possible side effects and secondary effects of this conflict? If this is a personal issue between two people, what will be the effect of intervening or not intervening? Will this issue continue to fester and grow, eventually pulling the entire department or organization into the fray? How could or will this issue affect your position or the perception of your managerial ability?

> Who will potentially gain from this conflict? Is this conflict actually a move to gain personal or organizational power? Are there other agendas at work here? Just as when you are preparing for organizational change, asking these questions will be valuable in formulating your response as a manager.

> Who stands to lose something as a result of this process? Who might lose their place and status? Whose status in the organization will be affected by the outcome? These questions will help you identify points of resistance that will surface as you move the principals into a resolution phase. This is also especially important in dealing with workplace bullying.

What could be the short- and long-term effects on the workplace? Will allowing this conflict to continue cause damage to the overall atmosphere or impair the quality of service or work flow? Will there need to be a systemic change as a result of resolving the conflict? Consider, for example, conflicts over work flow or patron service. You may need to assign additional training or adjust the current policies or procedures as a result of reaching a resolution. What sort of ripple effect will this resolution produce in other departments? Planning for the ripple effect can be critical when procedures and work flows are modified. Effective planning usually means consulting with members of other departments or units before final decisions are made or the implementation of the change has begun.

PUTTING IT ALL TOGETHER

Planning for conflict is like planning for any major organizational change, and therefore many of the principles of change management readily apply to the management of conflict. We need to focus on the following seven activities:

1. Be observant of the work environment and employees' personal styles as well as their reactions to various situations.

2. Watch for differing perceptions of work and different ways of approaching the organization's goals and objectives.

3. Develop a consistent managerial style that is conducive to communicating and effectively interacting with your employees and yourself. Be self-analytical and patient with yourself.

4. Recognize the dual nature of the workplace culture and learn to work within those public and private informational systems.

5. Understand that effective management is an ongoing process with the need for ongoing commitment on your part. Remember that there are no quick-fix solutions to most of these types of problems, and success is often realized in small increments.

6. Learn to manage the dynamics of workplace change and the many ways that it can affect your work environment. Develop a pattern and a method for affecting change in your workplace to which your staff can become accustomed.

7. Develop yourself into a position of leadership regardless of the scope of your managerial responsibility. Communicate, communicate, communicate!

NOTES

1. Survey respondent 451, public library staff, June 5, 2000.
2. Survey respondent 389, academic librarian, June 20, 2000.
3. Survey respondent 276, academic library staff, June 5, 2000.
4. Survey respondent 144, academic librarian, June 5, 2000; survey respondent 399, public librarian, June 4, 2000; survey respondent 411, academic librarian, June 5, 2000.
5. Survey respondent 112, academic library staff, June 6, 2000.
6. Survey respondent 343, public library staff, June 11, 2000.
7. Survey respondent 177, academic library director, June 6, 2000.

7

Examining Your
Organizational Culture

IN PLANNING FOR POTENTIAL CONFLICTS, MANAGERS MUST BE ABLE TO REC-
ognize, understand, and manage the type of organizational culture under
which their library operates. There are many models for organizational cultures that have received attention in the literature of business and industry,
all of which can help you identify what defines your particular culture. In
The Character of a Corporation, Rob Goffee and Gareth Jones define four
basic styles of organizational culture: *networked, mercenary, fragmented,* and
communal (1998, xiv). They offer a series of diagnostic tools to help pinpoint
which culture exists in a given place and time. One should pay careful attention to factors such as how the physical elements of the work environment are laid out, how and by whom communication is structured, how
communication flows within the organization, how work time is managed,
how people accomplish tasks, and how people identify themselves as individual working entities within the different parts of the organization. This
process involves an initial as well as an ongoing time investment on the part
of the supervisor, but the rewards are immense in terms of success within
that culture.

   Within each type of organizational culture there are both positive and
negative features and expressions of that culture. Each culture sends forth
a series of subtle messages that are internalized by all involved and, in turn,
become the basis of that culture. We will now examine each type of organizational culture using the definitions provided by Goffee and Jones.

THE NETWORKED CULTURE

A *networked* culture is characterized by the fact that "people know and like each other—they make friends, as the rule goes, all over the organization" (Goffee and Jones 1998, 73). This high level of socialization translates into a high degree of loyalty and an intense commitment to the organization and its goals. Significant value is placed on the ideal of reciprocity in human interactions, and a "We all look after each other" attitude is present. Such organizations often have an emphasis on ease of communication and acceptance of individual expression. Decisions tend to take longer than in some other models, but the degree of support for those decisions is often higher. Goffee and Jones suggest that in the networked culture, great value is placed on helping others in a selfless manner. This sometimes expresses itself well during organizational strain with other departments. People's willingness to pitch in and assist when needed, or even "helping before they are asked," is evident (1998, 81). This organizational atmosphere allows the institution to respond quickly and effectively to changes in the workplace. It is an adaptable culture.

Such an environment may have some qualities that seem ideal, but it is certainly not for every type of library or even every department within a library. Some people are not accustomed to a high degree of sociability and in fact may not feel comfortable in a networked culture. Similarly, individuals brought up with and rewarded for displaying a high degree of competitiveness may find the "Let's all work for each other" atmosphere frustrating and phony. They need the excitement of competition to spur them to achievement. It is important to note that this is not necessarily a personal flaw, but the networked culture is not a place where such a person can find satisfaction. The networked culture may be very effective in a library where service to patrons is an expressed organizational paradigm. Our survey indicated that many Technical Services (Acquisitions, Serials, and Cataloging) and Circulation departments gravitate toward the networked culture because their work flow and goals are interwoven, and there is a general service orientation to the work.

THE MERCENARY CULTURE

On the flip side is the *mercenary* culture, described as one most organizations readily admit exists for them, at least at certain times. Mercenary culture is "restless and ruthless" and includes the "hallmarks of high solidarity: strong, rather fierce, agreement around goals, a zest to get things done quickly, a powerful shared sense of purpose, a razor-sharp focus on goals and a certain boldness and courage about overcoming conflict and accepting the need to change" (Goffee and Jones 1998, 99).

Goffee and Jones admit that in a positive sense, the mercenary culture can be highly productive. Results and success are prized above all else. Employees are encouraged to compete, yet they work together to overwhelm any outside competition. This can take on the quality of a military campaign. Perceived adversaries may become problematic for a mercenary culture unless management clearly and continuously identifies the enemy in some productive fashion. A mercenary culture also will be in the throes of constant analysis and evaluation so as to retain its place "on the hill."

Mercenary cultures are also goal-driven cultures in which one campaign follows another. Although relatively few libraries, being traditionally service oriented, are mercenary in nature, they nevertheless have had a taste of the mercenary atmosphere as a result of rapid technological changes foisted upon them over the past thirty years. As soon as we recover from one wave of techno-fads and management innovation, another one comes along right behind it. Library administrators shamelessly compete with each other to see who can show off the trendiest gadgets first, implement the most radical ideas in organizing their staff, or dream up innovative services never before offered by libraries. It must be acknowledged that innovations and ideas are part of the responsibility of an administrator; that same administrator must recognize that these same innovations and ideas may have a profound effect on the organizational culture and, thus, plan for those changes. Such innovations often catapult library organizations from one type of culture to another. A library with a cooperative, networked culture may find itself radically transformed into a mercenary culture as a new innovation, major staff change, or organizational shift takes place. For example, if cross-functional "teams" are formed where before there had been hierarchal departments, confusion and dysfunction may last several years before people get used to the new ways of interacting. Budgetary shortfalls or increases will shift a culture if one group must compete with another for scarce or new resources. During such times, the level of networking and human interaction radically drops off as the competition intensifies. To many of the formerly networked people in the organization, this phase often seems like a world turned upside down; resistance takes on an intensity that matches the intensity of the change.

In a positive vein, if properly managed, the mercenary culture can shift without damage to accomplish a short-term goal that has been clearly identified and has had the groundwork established. As with managing change, managing an organizational shift, either temporarily or permanently, should be carefully planned, with the vision for change being clearly stated and passionately promoted throughout all chains of command on an ongoing basis throughout the process. The process must be monitored and adjusted so that the momentum and energy of the organization is turned toward the objectives rather than drained away in subversion and resistance.

The intense focus on results and success in a mercenary culture invariably leads to a situation of "winners and losers." In short, if an individual fails to perform, the results and penalties are swift. Goffee and Jones point out that a "mercenary culture's low sociability also brings with it a certain attractive ethos of fairness. Because of their absence of networks, politicking and cliques, mercenary cultures are usually meritocracies" (1998, 108).

This performance-based culture completely undermines the networked culture's system of building relationships to accomplish goals and secure positions within the organization. In an ideal mercenary culture, if an individual is not performing, is difficult, or is otherwise subverting a goal, he or she will not be given the period of leniency commonly found in networked cultures, where the intervention would be less direct and less embarrassing. In an ideal mercenary culture, insufficient performance or failure is understood to be fatal to the individual's career. The ideal mercenary culture would also be one free from the specter of litigation or workplace violence.

THE FRAGMENTED CULTURE

In a *fragmented* organizational culture, employees are "free agents" who have highly prized skills. They are in great demand and can rather easily get jobs elsewhere. This type of culture exists in fast-paced, high-risk organizations, such as investment banking, advertising, and in some high-technology fields. Goffee and Jones define this type of organizational culture as having "low sociability and low solidarity" (1998, 123). They also state that people in a fragmented culture "work at an organization but for themselves" (124). Although not many librarians would readily admit to working in such a culture, Goffee and Jones suggest it is a very common culture in educational and academic-based institutions where "your standing is also built on the outside world's assessment" (128). Within academic fields of study, one gains prestige based on personal development and intellectual production. Loyalty to colleagues or even the institution is a distant second to being valued by your subject-based peer network. This lack of appreciation for the values of a networked culture can also lead to a disdain for the need for cooperative efforts.

In a fragmented culture, attendance at meetings and planning sessions is often considered an obligation rather than something of value. Even leadership roles in this type of culture, such as that of an academic dean, may be viewed as an unwelcome, imposed assignment. Academic librarians, who have a dependent, service relationship to university faculty, may adopt the same fragmented culture posture and even in some cases develop a disdain for the service aspect of their profession. This disdain is often accentuated when individual librarians in academic library organizations have degrees beyond those considered terminal for the library profession. Significant interpersonal conflict can arise when credentials are compared and value judgments are made concerning who stands higher in the organizational pecking order. A librarian with a doctorate, for example, may imagine being above the routine activities of the everyday library world, preferring instead to focus on scholarship. Administrators often play a critical role in these conflicts because of the amount of value they place on academic credentials. One survey respondent resented "feeling like a second-class professional" when compared to colleagues with doctorates.[1] Such situations can be easily avoided if the chief university librarian takes the time to make certain each person's contribution is equally and publicly valued within the organization.

From our survey it appeared that academic librarians have the greatest difficulty with positive self-image because of the predominance of fragmented cultures in the halls of academia. However, as Goffee and Jones indicate, the overall culture honors "ideas, not individuals," and people may be hired for their intellect rather than their ability to get along and work well with others (1998, 128).

This trend has created a managerial system in higher education that is often highly dysfunctional. Thus exists the classic scenario of a cognitively brilliant individual who is hired for research and teaching but who later is "promoted" to a position of administrative responsibility. Such individuals are often asked to manage a culture that they barely comprehend and often do not appreciate. Ironically, too, the skills such scholars were prized for go to waste as they struggle to master a bureaucratic maze of university regulations and rules that seem meaningless compared to the important intellectual work to which they long to return. What usually lures rank-and-file professors to such choices is the extra "battle pay" that department head and other administrative positions include.

Goffee and Jones note that fragmented cultures can produce impressive results. There are, however, organizations with a negative form of fragmentation, "where low solidarity and low sociability are creating dysfunctional organizational outcomes. Other warning signs: pervasive cynicism, closed doors, difficulty in recruiting, and excessive critiquing of others. In other words, ideas may matter, but so do the people promoting them, and no one is safe" (1998, 131).

Not surprisingly, any of the above warning signs could be found in an academic library. It is critical to the future of academic librarianship that there is a balance between the university's culture and the internal culture of the library. Librarians in higher education should strive to avoid adoption of the negative features of the fragmented culture often promoted by their colleagues in the academic departments. Emulating the culture of the parent institution, in this instance, may create a psychologically damaging environment and engender conflicts that are very difficult to ever resolve. Academic librarians need to consider deliberately what cultural values prove most effective for their situation and their missions as librarians.

THE COMMUNAL CULTURE

Goffee and Jones identify their last form of organizational culture as *communal*, combining the competitive spirit of the mercenary culture with the work ethic of the networked culture. Communal cultures have an interest in results yet are concerned also with process and with people. There is a heavy focus on high sociability with a strong, almost religious sense of commitment on the part of managers and workers. Goffee and Jones use the example of a start-up company focused on one product. They observe that organizations with mercenary cultures may have communal cells within them (1998, 147).

Friendship and kindness are valued in a communal culture. The institution may openly refer to itself as "a family." In this culture, one walks the walks and talks the talk 24/7 as each member is required to embody the culture's ideals. All of this can, in a negative sense, take a heavy toll on one's life outside work. One of the authors of this book once worked for a sales unit that had a communal culture. The owner of the company served as an evangelist and constant promoter, setting the atmosphere for the entire operation. This was a private company, and the world revolved around the owner and his vision of reality. The employees were working to preserve a proud and distinguished heritage handed down by two preceding generations. The message was, "If you fail, we all fail." (On the negative side, if employees did not completely buy into this vision, they were seen as traitors.) The firm's employees were building a future for the company and themselves. Everything was focused on increasing sales. Anything else was a waste of precious time and energy. Employees were expected to attend all company parties and get-togethers. Many of those with families resented the intrusion into their personal lives. The insistence for complete organizational devotion finally drove so many good people away that the company went bankrupt.

Goffee and Jones suggest that a communal culture can exist for a time in an organization before morphing into another type of culture (1998, 176). Certainly, one might see a library adopting a communal culture when it is starting up or is the first of its kind in an area. Consider the settlement schools in eastern Kentucky at the turn of the century. Those people dedicated their lives and fortunes to making sure that this historic educational experiment was a success. Consider, too, Japanese work culture, which is communal and requires workers to go out with their colleagues almost every evening to engage in elaborate social activities designed to build solidarity.

Communal culture is very powerful because of the level of personal commitment required to make it function. According to our survey, some respondents believe that their library administrators strive for the commitment level of such a culture within their institutions. Communal culture does have its drawbacks, however. The intense focus on personality makes discipline and evaluations very difficult and unpleasant yet is absolutely necessary to retain the solidarity (Goffee and Jones 1998, 163).

In a communal culture, each person relies heavily upon nearby colleagues for just about everything. A downside to this type of organizational culture is that a failure of critical balance can lead to hero worship and a lack of critical thinking. A communal culture must constantly maintain its social and psychological ambience, and this activity may drain the organization's resources and thwart effective decision making, especially in a crisis.

Today's libraries face ever-changing organizational cultures. Whether your library tends toward a networked, mercenary, fragmented, or communal definition for its overall cultural orientation, it is possible to have several cultures existing under one roof, each affecting the other, for better or worse. As Riane Eisler states in her article on the concept of partnership as a managerial ideal, "Already, there are calls in the organizational-change literature for a recognition that we are interdependent on rather than independent of one another" (1995, 39). Eisler observes that many elements of our organizational cultures are entrenched and are traceable to our basic concepts of gender roles. Hence, they may be difficult and slow to change. However, at any level of an organization, a managerial plan for working with change events, personal or group transition, and their resulting conflicts in the context of the organizational culture cannot but have a positive impact on the rest of the institution. It can be considered an improved measure of a leader's professional vision. And it is certainly worth a sincere effort on our part as library professionals to understand our respective organizational cultures and to manage those culturally related conflicts in an informed fashion.

NOTE

1. Survey respondent 411, academic librarian, June 5, 2000.

8

Leadership:
So Much More
Than Management

THE ENCYCLOPEDIA OF LIBRARY HISTORY STATES THAT "THE TERMS 'ADMINIS-tration' and 'management' often have been used synonymously in the library field" (Wiegand and Davis 1994, 373). As has been demonstrated throughout this text, the intermingling of these concepts is flawed. The ability to "administer" the policies and procedures of an organization is only a part of the total package of managerial skills needed by today's librarian or manager. Historically, as Charles Williamson observed, "No one specifically connected the philosophy of library services with efficient library management" (Wiegand and Davis 1994, 374). Consequently, only recently did library science programs seriously concern themselves with the managerial aspects of librarianship. Professional library educational programs traditionally focus the curriculum on the achievement of technical skills with the idea that managerial skills will be learned, somehow, on the job. The question "What does any of this have to do with librarianship?" is commonly repeated both by our survey respondents and by colleagues we interact with at conferences and in the workplace. The image of a professional librarian apparently still does not include working well with others, in some people's view.

As library funding has fluctuated, costs for materials and resources have skyrocketed. Delivery of traditional as well as digital services has become the expectation rather than the exception, so more libraries have adopted an organizational posture similar to commercial businesses. Out of this stance have come increased expectations of accountability, measurable service results, and ever-increasing productivity. With the proliferation of online resources, librarians have found themselves trying to justify their very existence in this new information age. The traditional, passive "scholar in residence" approach to the profession and its attendant "let them come to us" attitude toward patrons have become quaint relics that actually work against the continued vitality of the library as a social institution. To survive and thrive in the new information age, we must move away from selecting our professional leadership on the basis of unrelated academic credentials and instead choose our leaders based on demonstrated managerial ability. To merely administer the affairs of a library has become a recipe for organizational disaster. As two well-known library consultants indicate, "The hyper speed of change in information services now demands libraries that are lean, mobile and strategic. They must be lean to meet expanding customer expectations within the confines of limited budgets; mobile to move quickly and easily with technological and other innovations; and strategic to anticipate and plan for market changes" (Schreiber and Shannon 2001, 36). Yet to rely on technical savvy alone to justify our existence will not provide us the future we desire but serves to create a role of subservience to those who sell and promote such products. Further, the responses from our survey as well as the ideas expressed in the current literature clearly indicate the need to develop and reward librarians who can administer, manage, and also provide leadership to their employees and institutions.

Leadership in modern Western European culture has a mythology and mystique surrounding it and is often thought to have quasi-magical origins. Leaders in the past were considered born to lead or given some special appointment by higher or divine powers. In reality, leadership has clearly been demonstrated to be, in many cases, a learned and practiced skill. Leadership trainers swarm the business world offering (often at considerable cost) workshops for managerial employees in this set of personal skills. What is surprising is that libraries often pay these fees without a clear picture of what the goals and objectives are for this training or for what constitutes leadership as opposed to management in a library organization.

It has become clear that we need to broaden the term *manager* to *leader* as the two can engender two very different connotations, and the term *leader* better defines the type of management style needed for effective management of conflict situations. What traits and characteristics constitute leadership as it relates to management? Leaders are able to articulate and communicate their often-original ideas and help others envision possibilities contained therein. They inspire, persuade, motivate, and challenge people to achieve the best possible results. They integrate themselves and their ideas into the organization in a skillful and politically savvy manner. They turn mistakes, conflicts, and failures into learning opportunities and shift focus away from scapegoating and assigning blame. They are able to effect change at the organizational level. Managers, on the other hand, as Donald E. Riggs indicates, "tend to work within defined bounds of known quantities; using well-established techniques to accomplish predetermined ends, the manager tends to stress means and neglect ends" (2001, 6). In the simplest terms, a managerial posture deals successfully with the known world, while leadership envisions and transcends the traditional boundaries to a goal beyond the process and procedure.

Leadership includes being willing to take risks. This does not mean that managerial skills and leadership are mutually exclusive; ideally, they work together. Like emotional intelligence's relationship to cognitive intelligence, they work in a balanced manner to produce optimal results.

In the world of professional librarianship, innovation and the change that must come as a result have not always been welcomed in an organizational culture focused on maintaining the status quo of previous generations. New and often successful innovations—like the idea of having a coffee shop or café in the library or the idea of twenty-four-hour access to reference services—are met with scorn and ridicule until the evidence for their success is overwhelming. The adherence to tradition has often thwarted the creative thinker or at least made change an uphill struggle. In recent years, technology has been the driving force in many library organizations. However, as Riggs points out, "The mission of libraries has not changed due to technology, but the way the mission is achieved has changed dramatically" (2001, 9). As was observed earlier in this book, constant adaptation and change have become the norm. This new paradigm has often resulted in major levels of interpersonal and organizational conflict. Riggs insists, "Library leaders must create an environment that embraces change not as a threat, but as an opportunity" (10). Leadership qualities as relayed in this statement reveal that the leader must envision the future and communicate that vision to others involved, stressing the way such changes can have a positive impact and thereby incorporating them into the momentum of the change event.

WHAT ARE THE OTHER QUALITIES OF LIBRARY LEADERSHIP?

Leaders know themselves. They use their strengths and acknowledge and work with their weaknesses. They self-evaluate and welcome the evaluations of others. Self-awareness is an absolutely critical feature. With these qualities, leaders can embrace change yet remain practical in the midst of chaos. They learn to manage the environment around them. In *Business Leadership*, author Viv Shackleton refers to this leadership skill as "impression management" and adds, "The leader acts in a way designed to create the impression among followers that he or she is competent" (1995, 103). Managing the world of perceptions and impressions around and about you requires acute self-analysis and honesty. As an analogy, proactively managing the impressions and perceptions surrounding you requires you to function as if you were a publicist in Hollywood. In short, you control the way you are perceived. The value of such an endeavor is directly related to your ability to influence, motivate, and inspire. Although many of us are taught as children to be self-effacing, knowing when to promote yourself and your ideas and when to promote the ideas of others can be critical to your success as a leader.

Leaders know how to allocate and manage money, read a ledger, and understand the concepts that surround effective financial management. Few innovations in a library can be realized without some expenditure or reallocation of often limited funds. Often, librarians are reluctant (or simply do not know how) to communicate their needs in terms of money. "Learn to speak the language of business and finance!" was the advice given by the late Murray S. Martin to one of the authors over dinner at a Charleston Conference in the 1990s. "Without being able to talk in the language of finance, you will almost never be able to convince higher management to invest in your idea" (personal communication). Those librarians wishing to be leaders must learn about such matters as fiscal cycles, budgeting, allocations, and reporting of financial matters. Being able to understand and work with finances gives you the ability to head off potential conflicts over money. Library leaders can then represent themselves to higher administration and know how, what, and when to speak of money to build credibility and ensure trust in their plans and projects. The library leader also understands the value of financial information that comes from below on the organizational scale. The leader cultivates an open-door policy that encourages staff to report issues and problems before they become serious.

When possible and appropriate, the library leader carries financial information back to the immediate work environment, allowing for an open and honest flow of communication about budget concerns. The last thing a leader wants is to learn of some financial problem after it is too late to remedy it. Management of allocated money must be a transparent process, and anyone who has undergone an internal audit understands this. The library leader builds relationships with those individuals who control the money at the institutional level and with the staff who monitor the financial activities of a department. As author Kate Donnelly Hickey states, "Leaders must forge imaginative and convincing links with their official funding and with alternative sources of revenue" (2001, 91).

Leaders realize the interconnected nature of events and relationships. They know that their words, ideas, and actions have consequences that move throughout their organization. Leaders make the time to analyze those connections and their possible impacts before they speak or act officially. In the management of conflict, a leader will take the time to digest all viewpoints, gather outside information as needed, and strategically plan a response. As we have seen before, this skill becomes critical when working with disciplinary actions or mediation of a dispute. Authors Becky Schreiber and John Shannon add that "leaders know it is important for the organization to be strategic, not just reactive" (2001, 47).

Leaders embrace diversity. This embracing moves beyond the barriers of gender, race, and social class. A leader will recruit, mentor, and promote a wide and diverse group of people to build the organization. Some staff may require a bit more effort to teach, educate, and encourage, but leaders make that extra effort. They know that building a diverse base in the library profession can only strengthen the profession as a whole. This may involve making opportunities for employees to help themselves through participation in workshops and seminars. It is also done through modeling the kinds of behaviors that you wish others to develop. This is, of course, leading by example and has been demonstrated to be very powerful in working with people from all backgrounds.

Leaders know how to acknowledge and accept the possibility of organizational failures as a normal part of work and learn to move beyond fault-finding to understanding the educational value of mistakes and errors. As we have seen in managing the conflict that often erupts during periods of organizational change, a leader of change must be able and willing to admit failures and be able to reframe that failure into a learning experience. A leader encourages staff to admit failures and acknowledge problems by the way he or she reacts to those revelations. If an employee knows that the problem or failure will be treated as something to be remedied and that his or her personal dignity will be respected and remain intact, the employee will be more likely to let the supervisor know about difficulties before they become major issues. Leaders know that sharing power is the quickest way to gain power and influence. If information is power, then sharing that information is more powerful. Anyone who tries to hoard information or resources is asking to be eventually bypassed and will quickly become nonessential. A leader also learns to cultivate trust among those for whom he is responsible. He or she learns that sharing power and responsibility provides for a dynamic and creative organization. The micromanager—who needs to know and control everything and everyone—is simply doomed to a life of frustration and eventual failure as a leader.

Leaders learn to have a vision of what is realistically possible and manage that vision in a practical, achievable manner. They also know how to sell that vision to others. There is a strong element of evangelical enthusiasm and old-fashioned salesmanship in the qualities of leadership. In a service-based profession like librarianship, being able to convey enthusiasm and dedication for services rendered creates an atmosphere of pride and excellence. It means letting others expand on your vision to further enhance the outcome. With regard to conflict management, you can sell the ideas of civility, mutual respect, and constructive conflict to your staff regardless of the type of environment you may have inherited. One survey respondent described how the current director had "transformed" a hostile, negative work environment into a place where "we look forward to coming to work."[1] The respondent revealed that this transformation was achieved over a period of a year by modeling positive behaviors and ways of handling conflict and by the personal leadership of the new director. It can be done if we are willing to make the effort.

Have you noticed something about the above-mentioned traits? A majority of the skills that we categorize as leadership qualities relate in some manner to the traits of emotional intelligence (EI). Daniel Goleman, in an article in the *Harvard Business Review*, states, "The most effective leaders are alike in one crucial way: they all have a high degree of what has come to be known as emotional intelligence" (1998, 92). Leaders, according to Goleman, all demonstrate the four basic EI skills (100):

1. Self-awareness
2. The ability to motivate themselves and others
3. A high degree of empathy for others shown by "thoughtfully considering other employees' feelings—along with other factors—in the process of making intelligent decisions"
4. A highly developed ability to manage social relationships

Leaders in librarianship are like leaders everywhere in that they fully understand the dynamics of the organizational environment and can operate successfully at both the cognitive and the emotional level. They are realistic visionaries who understand how to secure and evolve the organizational culture as they bring about different changes. They are entrepreneurial in approach and can work successfully to turn failed situations into success, to the benefit of all. They have a systemic view of the big picture and continually check the progress of their ideas, altering them as needed to achieve long-range goals. In referring to an earlier study about leadership in library organizations, Riggs wonders "why librarians do not like to talk more about leadership" (2001, 7). Riggs also predicts a coming crisis in leadership for libraries if librarians do not separate the qualities of good management from those of leadership and then mentor and cultivate colleagues who can transform our professional lives.

NOTE

1. Survey respondent 221, special librarian, June 9, 2000.

APPENDIX

Library Workplace Conflict Survey and Results

THE SURVEY BELOW WAS PLACED ON FIFTEEN LIBRARY ELECTRONIC discussion lists during the summer of 2000. During that time, more than 500 respondents from all walks of library life took the time to fill out the survey, and we have used the responses from 455 of these library professionals and staff throughout this book. We have tallied the responses to each question below, and the number of respondents for each appears in brackets next to the survey question. It should be stated clearly that the purpose and design of this survey was not to be a statistically valid instrument that would provide hard data for analysis. The sole purpose of the survey was to solicit personal commentary and anecdotes from the responders that would reflect their personal, subjective views of their workplace environments. This book places great value on those personal, subjective viewpoints as we feel it can accurately reflect how the individual will respond to his or her workplace situations. After all, with the large number of statistical surveys currently available on violence in the workplace, if statistical data alone could help individuals to identify and modify their behaviors, this book would probably never have been written as there would be no conflict in the workplace. With this survey, we decided to try to collect those personal views of reality, factually accurate or not, that form the actual basis for behavior.

A colleague of mine and I are currently writing a book on conflict in library organizations. We would like a few minutes of your time in helping gauge the climate of the modern library workplace.

This instrument is designed to survey your personal thoughts, attitudes and feelings about your position and your organization. It is a totally confidential document and your candidness will only improve the quality of the results. We also welcome your anecdotes and comments. No comments will be printed verbatim unless you specify, but will be paraphrased to protect your confidentiality. You'll notice that this survey uses informal language and asks for personal assessments. This is intentional in order to solicit as frank and candid a response as possible, not to follow the stricter guidelines and language of most traditional instruments.

Demographic Information

I. GENDER

a. Male [87]   [No answer, 12]
b. Female [356]

II. AGE

a. 20–29 [44]   d. 50–59 [135]
b. 30–39 [94]   e. 60+ [10]
c. 40–49 [163]   [No answer, 9]

III. EDUCATION

a. Less than undergrad [63]   e. PhD [14]
b. BA/BS [54]   f. Other [20]
c. MLS [222]   [No answer, 12]
d. MA + MLS [80]

IV. YEARS OF SERVICE IN LIBRARIES

a. 1–10 [139]   d. 30+ [36]
b. 11–20 [151]   [No answer, 23]
c. 21–30 [129]

V. IN YOUR INSTITUTION, WHAT IS YOUR OFFICIAL POSITION?

a. Faculty [139]   d. Other (*please specify*) [38]
b. Staff [194]   [No answer, 6]
c. Administrator or director [78]

VI. DO YOU, AS A PART OF YOUR POSITION, HAVE DIRECT SUPERVISION RESPONSIBILITIES?

a. Yes [281]   c. Not officially, but I do supervise [89]

b. No [66]   [No answer, 19]

The Workplace in General

(Check All That Apply)

I. WHY WERE YOU HIRED TO DO THIS JOB?

Academic credentials [268]

Experience in your area of specialization [271]

Experience in supervision/management   [155]

Other (*please specify*) [68]

II. WHY WAS YOUR SUPERVISOR/ADMINISTRATOR HIRED?

Academic credentials [175]

Experience in supervision/management [161]

Other (*please specify*) [153]

I do not know [4]

[No answer, 46]

III. IF YOU SUPERVISE, ANSWER QUESTIONS A THROUGH H. (IF YOU DON'T SUPERVISE, CHECK HERE [45] AND SKIP TO QUESTIONS I AND J.)

a. Are you comfortable with your role?

Yes [305]   No [36]   Other [7]

b. Do you feel you have adequate support from your superiors in matters of supervision?

Yes [280]   No [74]   Not applicable [19]

c. Do you feel you can adequately communicate with your superiors?

Yes [298]   No [64]   Not applicable [7]

d. Do you feel your subordinates have confidence in your capabilities as a supervisor?

Yes [319]   No [30]   [No answer, 6]

e. Do you feel you have good ability to be creative or innovative in your work and supervision?

Yes [286]   No [63]

f. Do you feel that the work you do is appreciated by your superiors?
    Yes [289]   No [72]   Not applicable [6]

g. Do you feel that the work you do is appreciated by your colleagues?
    Yes [276]   No [55]   Other [15]

h. Do you feel that the work you do is appreciated by your subordinates?
    Yes [290]   No [48]   Other [24]

i. Do you feel that you are satisfied with your interactions with your
    colleagues (those working at your same level)?
    Yes [330]   No [75]   Other [21]

j. Do you feel a genuine sense of accomplishment with your work and
    are satisfied with your professional life?
    Yes [357]   No [95]   Other [23]

IV. WITH REGARD TO YOUR LIBRARY'S ORGANIZATION

a. Are hard work and initiative valued?
    Yes [314]   No [124]   Other [13]   [No answer, 4]

b. Is there a sense of camaraderie among the staff?
    Yes [307]   No [115]   Other [20]   [No answer, 11]

c. What role does office/institutional politics play in your work life?
    (*Circle all that apply.*)
    1. It plays a role in my work life. [239]
    2. It plays a large role in my work life. [144]
    3. It does not play a role in my work life. [35]
    4. It has a positive impact on my work life. [67]
    5. It has a negative impact on my work life. [219]
    6. Other [14]

d. Describe the overall organizational climate in your workplace.
    1. Positive [162]   4. Other [15]
    2. Negative [159]   [No answer, 21]
    3. Neutral [98]

e. How would you characterize this climate? (*Circle all that apply.*)
    1. Supportive [227]
    2. Friendly [223]
    3. Ambivalent [152]
    4. Angry [98]
    5. Paranoid [125]
    6. Intimidating/inducing fear [97]

7. Combative [91]
8. Frustrating [235]
9. Tell us in your own words:_____
[No answer, 10]

  f. How would you describe the role administration plays in creating and maintaining this climate?

    1. Positive role [155]
    2. Neutral role [55]
    3. Negative role [112]
    4. Ambiguous role [119]
    5. Tell us in your own words:_____

Conflict in the Workplace

I. IS THERE INTERNAL ORGANIZATIONAL CONFLICT IN YOUR WORKPLACE?

Yes [360]   No [74]   [No answer, 21]

FREQUENTLY?

Yes [213]   No [184]   [No answer, 58]

II. WHO IS INVOLVED USUALLY? (*Rank 1 most often to 10 least often.*)

a. Staff against staff [189]
b. Staff against supervisor [150]
c. Supervisor against staff [119]
d. Librarian against librarian [127]
e. Faction against faction [110]

f. Librarian against administrator [124]
g. Administrator against librarian [95]
h. Administrator against staff [90]
i. Staff against administrator [84]
j. Others (*please specify*)

III. DO PROBLEMS FROM THE PERSONAL LIVES OF THOSE AT WORK, INCLUDING YOURSELF, EVER MAKE AN APPEARANCE IN THE WORKPLACE?

Yes [428]   No [27]

IF SO, HOW OFTEN?

a. Often [110]
b. Sometimes [192]

c. Not often [149]
d. Never [4]

IV. WHAT IMPACT DO PERSONAL PROBLEMS HAVE ON THE WORKPLACE?

a. Distracting [314]
b. Time-consuming [264]
c. Causes conflict [134]
d. Tell us in your own words:_____

V. WHAT FORMS DO THE PERSONAL PROBLEMS TAKE?
(*Rank 1 most often to 5 least often.*)

a. Verbal debate [286]   Rank _____
b. Verbal shouting [102]   Rank _____
c. Written communication (includes e-mail) [229]   Rank _____
d. Silent treatment [272]   Rank _____
e. Group argument [140]   Rank _____

VI. HAS AN ACT OF PHYSICAL VIOLENCE EVER TAKEN PLACE AT WORK?

Yes [57]   No [398]

VII. WHAT FORM DID THE VIOLENCE TAKE? (*Check all that apply.*)

Physical assault [20]   Other (*please specify*) [14]
Verbal threats [49]   [No answer, 122]
Items thrown [27]

VIII. WERE POLICE SUMMONED?

Yes [27]   No [30]

IX. WERE LEGAL ACTIONS TAKEN?

Arrests [5]   Other (*please specify*) [51]
Summons [1]

X. WHAT HAPPENED AS A RESULT OF ALL OF THIS?
(*Tell us in your own words.*)

XI. WHO TAKES A ROLE IN HELPING TO RESOLVE YOUR CONFLICTS? (*Check all that apply.*) THEN RANK THEIR EFFECTIVENESS IN HELPING TO RESOLVE THE CONFLICTS.
(*Rank 1 most effective to 6 least effective.*)

1. Only those directly involved [267]   Rank _____
2. Supervisor [285]   Rank _____
3. Administrator [191]   Rank _____
4. Institutional counselors/mediators [73]   Rank _____
5. A group of peers [98]   Rank _____
6. Other (*please specify*) [29]   Rank _____

XII. WHAT COULD BE DONE TO REDUCE CONFLICT IN YOUR ORGANIZATION?

XIII. IS THERE ANYTHING YOU WISH TO ADD (A STORY OF CONFLICT OR RESOLUTION)?

REFERENCES

AAUP (American Association of University Professors). The American Association of University Professors: Academic freedom for a free society. http://www.aaup.org/aboutaaup/description.htm.

Abernathy, Karling Clymer. 2002. Union and management at the Rapid City Public Library. *Public Libraries* 41:139.

Abraham, Rebecca. 1999. Emotional intelligence in organizations: Conceptualizing the roles of self-esteem and job-induced tension. *Leadership and Organization Development Journal* 1(20): 18–25.

Anderson, Renee N., John D'Amicantonio, and Henry DuBois. 1992. Labor unions or professional organizations: Which have our first loyalty? *College and Research Libraries* 53:331–40.

Appalachian State University, Human Resource Services. Frequently asked questions regarding the HIPAA privacy rule. http://www1.appstate.edu/dept/hrs/forms/hipaaquestions.pdf.

Ashforth, Blair E., and Ronald H. Humphrey. 1995. Emotion in the workplace: A reappraisal. *Human Relations* 48:99–125.

Auld, Hampton (Skip). 2002. The benefits and deficiencies of unions in public libraries. *Public Libraries* 41:135.

Bacal, Robert. 1998. Work911/Bacal & Associates/Dealing with hostile bait. http://www.work911.com/articles/hostilebait.htm.

Becvar, Raphael J., and Dorothy S. Becvar. 1982. *Systems theory and family therapy: A primer.* Lanham, MD: University Press of America.

Beer, Jennifer E., and Eileen Stief. 1997. *The mediator's handbook.* 3rd ed. Gabriola Island, British Columbia: New Society.

Bencivenga, Dominic. 1999. Dealing with the dark side. *HR Magazine* 44:50–58.

195

Bernstein, Albert J., and Sydney Craft Rozen. 1992. *Neanderthals at work: How people and politics can drive you crazy . . . and what you can do about them.* New York: Wiley.

Bing, Stanley. 2000. *What would Machiavelli do? The ends justify the meanness.* New York: HarperBusiness.

Bowen, Brayton R. 2000. *Recognizing and rewarding employees.* New York: McGraw-Hill.

Braunstein, Susan. 2002. Thoughts on unions in public libraries. *Public Libraries* 41:138–39.

Bridges, William. 1991. *Managing transitions: Making the most of change.* Reading, MA: Addison-Wesley.

Brust, Beth Wagner. 2001. *Emotional intelligence leader's guide.* Carlsbad, CA: CRM Learning.

Carroll, Holly, and Linda Klancher. 2002. Labor unions in public libraries: A perspective from both sides of the issue. *Public Libraries* 41:138.

Casey, James B. 2002. Beware of what you wish for! *Public Libraries* 41:137–38.

Caudron, Shari. 1999. The hard case for soft skills. *Workforce* 78:60–66. Retrieved from http://hr.monster.com/articles/hardcase/.

Chapman, Elwood N., and Sharon Lund O'Neil. 1999. *Your attitude is showing.* 9th ed. Upper Saddle River, NJ: Prentice Hall.

Chavez, Larry. 2002. Workplace violence . . . what a CEO can do to reduce the risk of workplace violence. http://members.aol.com/endwpv/ceo-info.html.

Cherniss, Cary, and Daniel Goleman, eds. 2001. *The emotionally intelligent workplace: How to select for, measure, and improve emotional intelligence in individuals, groups, and organizations.* San Francisco: Jossey-Bass.

Coccia, Cynthia. 1998. Avoiding a toxic organization. *Nursing Management* 29:32–33.

Cohen, Moshe. 1998. Managing workplace conflict requires a delicate diplomacy. *Boston Business Journal* 18:19.

Constantine, Madonna G., and Kathy A. Gainor. 2001. Emotional intelligence and empathy: Their relation to multicultural counseling knowledge and self awareness. *Professional School Counseling* 5:131–37.

Conti, Adam J. 1997. The workplace and the Internet: Resources, risks, privacy and opportunities—maintaining employment records electronically. http://www.contilaw.com/articles/interwork.html.

Cooper, Robert, and Ayman Sawaf. 2001. Emotional intelligence in leadership organizations. http://www.feel.org/articles/cooper_sawaf.html.

Csikszentmihalyi, Mihaly. 1997. *Finding flow: The psychology of engagement with everyday life.* New York: Basic.

Daly, Kathleen Evans. 2002. A better way of bargaining. *Public Libraries* 41:135–36.

Dana, Daniel. 2001. *Conflict resolution: Mediation tools for everyday worklife.* New York: McGraw-Hill.

DesRoches, Brian. 1995. *Your boss is not your mother: Breaking free from emotional politics to achieve independence and success at work.* New York: Morrow.

Deutsch, Morton, and Peter T. Coleman, eds. 2000. *The handbook of conflict resolution: Theory and practice.* San Francisco: Jossey-Bass.

Dickter, Laurence S. 2002. Empowering library workers through collective bargaining. *Public Libraries* 41:141.

Domenici, Kathy, and Stephen W. Littlejohn. 2001. *Mediation: Empowerment in conflict management.* 2nd ed. Prospect Heights, IL: Waveland.

Drucker, Peter F. 1999. *Management challenges for the 21st century.* New York: HarperBusiness.

Eisler, Riane. 1995. From domination to partnership: The hidden subtext of organization change. *Training and Development* 49:32–40.

Elgin, Suzette Haden. 1980. *The gentle art of verbal self-defense.* Paramus, NJ: Prentice Hall.

Employee Assistance Providers/MN. Quoted on Aardvarc.org. http://www.aardvarc.org/dv/statistics.shtml.

EQ Institute. What others say about feelings. http://www.eqi.org/others.htm.

Garcha, Rajinder, and John C. Phillips. 2001. U.S. academic librarians: Their involvement in union activities. *Library Review* 50:122–27.

Gibbs, Nancy R. 1995. The EQ factor. *Time* 146:60–66.

Goffee, Rob, and Gareth Jones. 1998. *The character of a corporation: How your company's culture can make or break your business.* New York: HarperBusiness.

Goleman, Daniel. 1994. *Emotional intelligence: Why it can matter more than IQ.* New York: Bantam.

———. 1998. What makes a leader? *Harvard Business Review* 76:92–102.

Guyton, Theodore Lewis. 1975. *Unionization: The viewpoint of librarians.* Chicago: American Library Association.

Hickey, Kate Donnelly. 2001. Financial resources and what leaders should know. *Journal of Library Administration* 32:81–93.

Hoadley, Irene B. 1999. Reflections: Management morphology—how we got to be who we are. *Journal of Academic Librarianship* 25:267.

Hovekamp, Tina Maragou. 1994. Organizational commitment of professional employees in union and nonunion research libraries. *College and Research Libraries* 55:297–307.

Huy, Quy Nguyen. 1999. Emotional capability, emotional intelligence, and radical change. *Academy of Management Review* 24:325–45.

James, Johnnie A. 1997. Balancing employers' workplace violence concerns with the rights of the psychologically disabled under the ADA: Direct threat and the individual's right to privacy. http://www.alschuler.com/print/artjaj.html.

Johnson, Cameron. 2002. Professionalism, not paternalism. *Public Libraries* 41:139–40.

Johnson, Carol French. 2002. Union staff and customer service: Do they collide? *Public Libraries* 41:136–37.

Johnson, Carol French, and Cathy Bremer. 2002. Can unions solve the low-pay dilemma? *American Libraries* 33:65–69.

Johnson, Dennis L. 1994. A team approach to threat assessment. *Security Management* 38:73–77.

Johnson, Pamela R., and Julie Indvik. 2001. Rudeness at work: Impulse over restraint. *Public Personnel Management* 30:457–65.

Join Together Online. 1999a. New study shows 1 in 4 angry at work. http://www .jointogether.org/gv/news/summaries/reader/0,2061,260114,00.html.

———. 1999b. Workplace violence continues to increase. http://www .jointogether.org/gv/news/summaries/reader/0,2061,260832,00.html.

———. 2002. 18 workplace violence incidents since September 11th: For the workplace killer, it is business as usual. http://www.jointogether.org/gv/news/ alerts/reader/0,2061,551473,00.html.

Julius, Daniel J., J. Victor Baldridge, and Jeffrey Pfeffer. 1999. A memo from Machiavelli. *Journal of Higher Education* 70:113–33.

Kaufer, Steve, and Jurg W. Mattman. 2001. Workplace violence: An employer's guide. http://www.noworkviolence.com//articles/employers_guide.htm.

Kouzes, James M., and Barry Z. Posner. 1995. *The leadership challenge: How to keep getting extraordinary things done in organizations.* San Francisco: Jossey-Bass.

Kowalski, Robin M., ed. 2001. *Behaving badly: Aversive behaviors in interpersonal relationships.* Washington, DC: American Psychological Association.

Laabs, Jennifer. 1999. Emotional intelligence at work. *Workforce* 78:68–71.

LaFasto, Frank, and Carl Larson. 2001. *When teams work best: 6,000 team members and leaders tell what it takes to succeed.* Thousand Oaks, CA: Sage.

Lewicki, Roy J., David M. Saunders, and John W. Minton. 2001. *Essentials of negotiation.* 2nd ed. Boston: McGraw-Hill/Irwin.

Lilore, Doreen. 1984. *The local union in public libraries.* Hamden, CT: Library Professional Publications.

Lynch, Mary Jo. Collective bargaining agreements and pay systems. 1997. American Library Association, Office for Research and Statistics. http://www.ala.org/ala/hrdr/libraryempresources/collectivebargaining.htm.

Masters, Marick F., and Robert R. Albright. 2002. *The complete guide to conflict resolution in the workplace.* New York: AMACOM.

Mattman, Jurg W. 2003. Positive steps for screening out workplace violence. http://www.noworkviolence.com/articles/screening_out_workplace.htm.

McConnell, Campbell R., and Stanley L. Brue. 2002. *Microeconomics: Principles, problems and policies.* Boston: McGraw-Hill/Irwin.

Metz, Ruth F. 2001. *Coaching in the library: A management strategy for achieving excellence.* Chicago: American Library Association.

Montoya, Paul. 1997. Workplace violence still top concern among businesses. *San Antonio Business Journal* 10:18.

Moxnes, Paul. 1999. Deep roles: Twelve primordial roles of mind and organization. *Human Relations* 52:1427–44.

Namie, Gary, and Ruth Namie. 2000. *The bully at work: What you can do to stop the hurt and reclaim your dignity on the job.* Naperville, IL: Sourcebooks.

National Victim Assistance Academy. 1998. Chapter 21, Section 3: Workplace violence: Its nature and extent. http://www.ojp.usdoj.gov/ovc/assist/nvaa /ch21-3wk.htm.

O'Keefe, Terry. 1998. Emotional skills give execs an edge in the workplace. http://www.bizjournals.com/atlanta/stories/1998/10/26/smallb6.html.

O'Reilly, Robert C., and Marjorie I. O'Reilly. 1981. *Librarians and labor relations: Employment under union contracts.* Westport, CT: Greenwood.

Pease, Barbara. 1995. Workplace violence in libraries. *Library Management* 16:30–39.

Petrini, Catherine, and Kenneth Hultman. 1995. Scaling the wall of resistance. *Training and Development Journal* 49:15–18.

Poe, Randall, and Carol Lee Courter. 1996. Staff conflicts. *Across the Board* 33:5.

Rhodes, Daniel, and Kathleen Rhodes. 1998. *Vampires: Emotional predators who want to suck the life out of you.* Amherst, NY: Prometheus.

Riggs, Donald E. 2001. The crisis and opportunities in library leadership. *Journal of Library Administration* 32:5–17.

Rubin, Harriet. 1997. *The princessa: Machiavelli for women.* New York: Dell.

Ryan, Kathleen D., and Daniel K. Oestreich. 1991. *Driving fear out of the workplace: How to overcome the invisible barriers to quality, productivity, and innovation.* San Francisco: Jossey-Bass.

Ryback, David. 1998. *Putting emotional intelligence to work: Successful leadership is more than IQ.* Boston: Butterworth-Heinemann.

Salovey, Peter, and J. D. Mayer. 1993. The intelligence of emotional intelligence. *Intelligence* 17:433–42.

Schechter, Harriet. 2000. *Conquering chaos at work.* New York: Simon and Schuster.

Schmidt, Warren H., and B. J. Gallagher Hateley. 2001. *Is it right to always be right?* New York: AMACOM.

Schreiber, Becky, and John Shannon. 2001. Developing library leaders for the 21st century. *Journal of Library Administration* 32:35–57.

Shackleton, Viv. 1995. *Business leadership*. London: Routledge.

Spang, Lothar. 1993. Collective bargaining and faculty status: A twenty-year case study of Wayne State University librarians. *College and Research Libraries* 54:241–53.

Sparanese, Ann C. 2002. Unions in libraries: A positive view. *Public Libraries* 41:140–41.

Steingold, Fred S. 1997. *The employer's legal handbook: A complete guide to your legal rights and responsibilities*. Berkeley: Nolo.

———. 2003. *The employer's legal handbook: A complete guide to your legal rights and responsibilities*. Berkeley: Nolo.

Strathern, Paul. 1998. *Machiavelli in 90 minutes*. Chicago: Ivan R. Dee.

Straus, David. 2002. *How to make collaboration work: Powerful ways to build consensus, solve problems, and make decisions*. San Francisco: Berrett-Koehler.

Todaro, Julie. 1999. Reasonable expectation of adult behavior. *Library Administration and Management* 13:15–17.

U.S. Department of Labor, Employee Benefits Security Administration. Fact sheet: Health Insurance Portability and Accountability Act (HIPAA). http://www.dol.gov/ebsa/newsroom/fshipaa.html.

Violent employees: Cues, clues and constructive responses. 1996. *Getting Results . . . for the Hands-On Manager* 41:6–7.

Wagner, Pat. 1999. *Avoiding the conflict trap* [audiocassette]. Denver, CO: Pattern Research.

Weatherford, John W. 1988. *Librarians' agreements: Bargaining for a heterogeneous profession*. Metuchen, NJ: Scarecrow.

Weber, Mark W. 1992. Support staff unions in academic and public libraries: Some suggestions for managers with reference to the Ohio experience, 1984–1990. *Journal of Library Administration* 17:65–86.

Weisinger, Hendrie. 1998. *Emotional intelligence at work: The untapped edge for success*. San Francisco: Jossey-Bass.

Wiegand, Wayne A., and Donald G. Davis, eds. 1994. *Encyclopedia of library history*. New York: Garland.

Wilkinson, John Provost, and Margaret Ann Wilkinson. 1997. Plotting conflict. *Library Administration and Management* 11:204–16.

Williams, Virginia Parrott, and Redford Williams. 1998. *Lifeskills*. New York: Random House.

Willits, Robert. 1999. When violence threatens the workplace: Personnel issues. *Library Administration and Management* 11:166–71.

Winslade, John, and Gerald Monk. 2000. *Narrative mediation: A new approach to conflict resolution*. San Francisco: Jossey-Bass.

Yankelovich, Daniel. 1999. *The magic of dialogue: Transforming conflict into cooperation*. New York: Simon and Schuster.

INDEX

JACK G. MONTGOMERY earned his MLS at the University of Maryland–College Park in 1987. He has worked in academic law libraries in Virginia, Ohio, and Missouri. In 1998, Montgomery made the transition to the general academic library and to Western Kentucky University, where he is an associate professor/collection services coordinator. He writes and edits regular columns for *Against the Grain* and serves on the editorial boards of *Against the Grain* and *Library Resources and Technical Services*. He has been speaking professionally at AALL and Charleston Conference programs since 1989 and at ALA and regional programs since 1999. Montgomery also conducts professional seminars on emotional intelligence to library groups nationwide.

ELEANOR I. COOK is serials coordinator and professor at Belk Library, Appalachian State University, Boone, North Carolina, where she has worked since 1990. Prior to this, she served as serials catalog librarian at North Carolina State University and Georgia Institute of Technology. She began her library career at the University of North Carolina–Chapel Hill as a paraprofessional. She received her MSLS in 1982 and earned an MA in Leadership and Educational Studies from Appalachian in 1994. Cook is active in various national and regional library associations. She was the president of the North American Serials Interest Group (NASIG) in 2002/3. She is chief editor of the electronic discussion list ACQNET-L and serves on the editorial boards of *Against the Grain* and *The Serials Librarian*.